Keys to Success at School and Beyond

7 Tips for Study Skills: Oxford Graduate Reveals the Secrets of Success

Mehdi Toozhy
BSC.(HONS.), MSC, SCIENTIFIC RESEARCHER

Suite 300 - 990 Fort St
Victoria, BC, Canada, V8V 3K2
www.friesenpress.com

Copyright © 2014 by Mehdi Toozhy
First Edition — 2014

keystosuccessatschool.com

All rights reserved. No part of this publication may be reproduced, distributed, or transmitted in any form or by any means, including photocopying, recording, or other electronic or mechanical methods, without the prior written permission of the publisher, except in the case of brief quotations embodied in critical reviews and certain other noncommercial uses permitted by copyright law.

ISBN
978-1-4602-5223-9 (Hardcover)
978-1-4602-5224-6 (Paperback)
978-1-4602-5225-3 (eBook)

1. *Education, Study Skills*

Distributed to the trade by The Ingram Book Company

LEARNING NEVER EXHAUSTS THE MIND.
—LEONARDO DA VINCI

....

TO CONCERNED PARENTS:
THIS IS THE PEACE OF MIND YOU ARE SEEKING.
—MEHDI TOOZHY

Table of Contents

Acknowledgements .... **xiii**

Preface **1**

First Key:
Discover Your Learning Style **3**
    Introduction 4
    1.1 What Is Intelligence? 4
    1.2 Understand Your Intelligence 5
    1.3 Strengthening Your Intelligence 11
        1.3.1 Visual Learners 12
        1.3.2 Physical Learners 12
        1.3.3 Musical Learners 13
        1.3.4 Interpersonal Learners or Social Intelligence 14
        1.3.5 Introvert or Intrapersonal Learners 15
        1.3.6 Logical Learners 17
        1.3.7 Language Learners 18
    1.4 Setting a Goal for Yourself 19

  1.4.1 Academic Grades *20*
  1.4.2 Social Life *21*
  1.4.3 Sports and Exercise *21*
  1.4.4 Family *22*
  1.4.5 Overcoming Stress *22*
  1.4.6 Long-term Goals *23*
  1.4.7 Happiness *23*
 1.5 How Great Minds Viewed Intelligence 24
 1.6 A Lesson from My Learning Style 25
 Exercises 26

Second Key:
Learn to Cope with Stress 29
 Introduction 30
 2.1 What Is Your Personal Image? 30
  Exercise *32*
 2.2 Media Influence 33
  Exercise *33*
 2.3 Academic Pressure 34
  2.3.1 Managing Time *34*
  2.3.2 Organize Yourself *35*
  2.3.3 Create a Good Studying Environment *36*
  2.3.4 Exam Fever *36*
 2.4 Steps to Reduce Your Stress 39
  2.4.1 Diet *40*
  2.4.2 The Power of Music *41*
  2.4.3 The Power of Water *42*
  2.4.4 The Power of Writing Your Thoughts *42*
 2.5 How Great Minds Viewed Stress 43
 Exercises 44

Third Key:
Friends and Competition 47
 Introduction 48

3.1 WHY IS IT IMPORTANT WHO YOU BEFRIEND?.... 48
3.2 COMMUNICATION SKILLS......................... 49
3.3 HOW TO CHOOSE A FRIEND...................... 50
3.4 MY PERSONAL EXPERIENCE 51
3.5 HOW GREAT MIND VIEWED FRIENDSHIP......... 53
3.6 RECOMMENDED BOOKS AND MAGAZINES 54
EXERCISES.. 55

FOURTH KEY:
DON'T GIVE UP 57
INTRODUCTION... 58
4.1 WHY YOU NEED PERSISTENCE.................... 58
4.2 HOW TO DEVELOP YOUR PERSISTENCE 59
    4.2.1 Keeping a Positive Mind............................60
    4.2.2 Keep Trying...60
    4.2.3 Keep a Role Model...................................61
4.3 INSPIRATION FROM NATURE..................... 62
4.4 HOW GREAT MINDS VIEWED SUCCESS 65
4.5 MY EXPERIENCE 67
EXERCISES... 68

FIFTH KEY:
EXPAND YOUR LEARNING CAPACITY 71
INTRODUCTION... 72
5.1 WHY YOU SHOULD EXPAND YOUR LEARNING
CAPACITY 73
5.2 PRACTICAL STEPS TO EXPAND YOUR LEARNING
CAPACITY 74
    5.2.1 Seek New Activities..................................74
    5.2.2. Think Creatively...................................75
    5.2.3 Socialize..77
5.3 PRESENTATION SKILLS 78
5.4 TEAM WORK SKILLS 81
5.5 HOW TO UNDERSTAND A CONCEPT 83

5.6 Practice Self-education............................ 86
    5.6.1 Eight Techniques that Stimulate Self-education 86
    5.6.2 Resources for Self-education 91
5.7 How Great Minds Viewed Learning.......... 91
5.8 My Experience 94
Exercises.. 94

Sixth Key:
How to Approach a Problem 99
Introduction... 100
6.1 The Power of Your Subconscious Mind.... 100
6.2 How to Practice Subconscious Problem Solving 102
6.3 How to Approach Math and Physics Problems... 102
6.4 Ask the Three Questions 103
6.5 How to Approach a Project 105
6.6 Critical Thinking Skills 107
6.7 How Great Minds Viewed Problems......... 107
    6.7.1 Thomas Alva Edison 108
    6.7.2 Albert Einstein 108
    6.7.3 Henry Ford 109
Exercises 110

Seventh Key:
How to Discover Your Own Path 113
Introduction... 114
7.1 How to Discover Your Passion............... 114
7.2 How Great Minds Discovered Their Paths. 117
7.3 EINSTEIN SECRET MESSAGE TO HIS SON 119
Exercises 119

References 123

DEDICATED TO MY DEAR WIFE, SABA

Acknowledgements

This book is the essence of ten years of studies at three international universities. Upon entering the Danish Technical University, I began to search for techniques to improve how I learned. I always looked for students in their final semester and asked for their feedback and notes. I studied these notes carefully and managed to build a knowledge base that I put into practice in my own studies. I compiled these many years' worth of notes and observations, and it resulted in the production of this book. It is not easy to study. I have seen many students give up on their dreams because they felt overwhelmed and lonely.

I decided to write this book to encourage those who feel they can't continue because they fear they lack the talent to succeed.

I learned that you have to earn knowledge by hard work.

I am grateful to the Creator for being able to finish this work.

I would like to thank one of my great teachers, Professor Arvid Andersen from the Danish Technical University in Denmark, for his great advice and help in my journey to become an engineer.

I would also like to extend my thanks to my family for supporting and encouraging me to finish this book.

This book is for all students who seek to realize their dreams.

Preface

What is the purpose of this book?

It was written to make you realize your true potential and help you to achieve it.

The idea of writing this book came to me when I realized that if I knew in university what I know now, life back then would have been much more enjoyable. I decided to write this book so that when you have finished the academic part of your life, you don't look back and say, "I wish somebody had told me about that." Knowing is a very powerful thing, and I will help you to know.

When you start your college or university journey you will face many challenges. It is hard to find someone to tell you what to do. The feeling of information overload is overwhelming, and you may feel saturated at the very beginning. You have to live by yourself and deal with the challenges that life throws at you.

In the 10 years of my academic life I experienced three different educational systems:

- Danish
- British
- German Engineering Standard

My approach to studying at university is a combination of my many years of international experience. This book reflects the techniques that made me successful all those years.

My quest for science at an early age led me to move to Europe alone when I was a grade 8 student so I could seek new experiences. Keeping a positive mind and treating every experience as part of life's classroom enriched me and helped me to forget difficult and lonely times. My knowledge expanded with every problem encountered, and over time, things became easier and I got better at problem solving.

I decided to write this book in a way that is easy to read and with clear messages rather than writing a detailed description of study techniques that would be tiring and time consuming. I want you to think smart and consider the big picture. Once you have the main idea, looking for and researching information should be the easy part. I will show you the direction you need to take, but you have to take the steps and show commitment to ensure you reach your goal.

Whenever I use a quote from great minds it confirms my own experiences. You can apply these experiences and take comfort in knowing that you can be a successful student and also continue to be successful in your professional life. As a nature lover, I have also researched and presented you with inspiration from nature.

My motto is: "Try to learn from everyone and everything in your life journey."

In other words, try to treat everyday life as a university.

The Keys to Success at School and Beyond is a book that will help you to overcome challenges and remind you that human beings are very powerful when they put their minds into making the world a better place. Students who say that they don't have the talent to succeed need to know that they are the only ones who can help themselves. So stand up and know that hard work is even more important than talent.

First Key:
Discover Your Learning Style

Nothing in life is to be feared, it is only to be understood. Now is the time to understand more, so that we may fear less.
—Marie Curie, Scientist (1867 – 1934)

Topics in this section:

- What is Intelligence?
- Understand Your Intelligence
- Strengthening Your IntelligenceSetting a Goal for Yourself
- How Great Minds Viewed Intelligence
- A Lesson from My Learning Style

Introduction

I have often heard from students that they don't have the talent or intelligence to excel at school, college, or university. It seems to me that a large number of students suffer from this illusion. Two of my aims for writing this book are to clarify the understanding of intelligence and to share my experience and knowledge with you. Anybody that wants to be successful at school has to learn to appreciate their unique way of learning things. Behind any great success lies one fundamental that I can say worked for me through my 10 years at university: Hard work is more important than talent.

1.1 What Is Intelligence?

Intelligence isn't just about how many levels of science courses you've taken, how fast you can solve an algorithm, or how many vocabulary words you command. It's about being able to approach a new problem, recognize its important components, and solve it, and then taking that knowledge gained and putting it towards solving the next, more complex problem. It's about innovation and imagination and about being able to put that to use to make the world a better place.

1.2 Understand Your Intelligence

There are many types of intelligence. The idea is that each one of us is unique in nature, and we are all able to accomplish the desired goals in our life. If we set specific goals and establish steps towards accomplishing those goals, then there is no reason why we should not be able to achieve what we desire. Howard Gardner is best known for his theory of multiple intelligences as outlined in his book *Frames of Mind: The Theory of Multiple Intelligences* (1983). He proposed the different types of intelligence that lend themselves to multiple learning styles.

In the following, I will go through different types of learners. This is not necessarily a comprehensive list, but rather only seven out of many kinds of learners. I hope this will demonstrate that any type of intelligence is valuable and can achieve great potential once it is appreciated and used in the right manner to achieve a goal.

The seven types of learners:

1. Visual learners

They think in pictures and need to see things to understand them. They learn better when ideas are presented in diagrams, films, and charts.

2. Physical learners

Those who have high "bodily-kinesthetic" intelligence are said to be good at body movement, performing actions, and physical control. Employing simple physical engagement, such as taking notes and building models, can help them learn faster.

3. Musical learners

They learn by reading aloud and giving rhythm to the information they are learning.

4. Interpersonal learners or social learners

They learn by interacting with others. They learn best when studying in a group of several students.

5. Intrapersonal or introvert learners

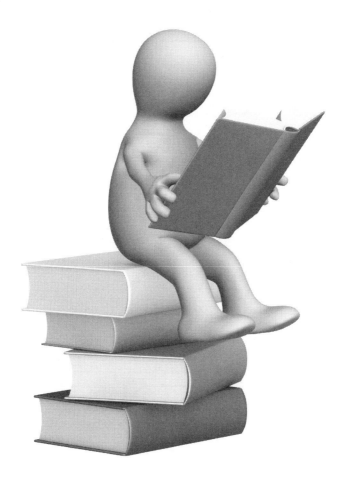

In a team, they work independently and then join with others once they have completed their part of the project.

6. Logical learners

They are math thinkers. They learn by reasoning, using numbers, and critical thinking. They are pattern finders.

7. Language learners

People with high "verbal-linguistic" intelligence display a facility with words and languages. They are typically good at reading, writing, telling stories, and memorizing words. They struggle with math.

We learn by more than one method. In this book, I will provide many tips for any type of learner.

1.3 Strengthening Your Intelligence

Once you've discovered your learner's individual mix of strengths, you can begin tailoring your learning methods. There are a number of ways to accomplish this, but it helps to begin with an overview of general strategies for engaging each kind of intelligence.

1.3.1 Visual Learners

People with a strong visual intelligence remember things visually, including exact sizes and shapes of objects. They like posters, charts, and graphic presentations. They like any kind of visual clues. They enjoy drawing.

Here are some ways to strengthen your visual intelligence:

- Write a language experience story and then illustrate it with pictures.
- Study and create maps, diagrams, and graphs.
- Write a word on the blackboard with a wet finger. Visualize the word as it disappears. Try to spell it afterwards.
- Take a survey. Put the information in a chart.
- Write words vertically.
- Cut out words from a magazine and use them in a letter.
- Use pictures to stimulate reading or writing.
- Use colorful newspapers and magazines when reading.

1.3.2 Physical Learners

People who have a strong body movement intelligence like to move, dance, wiggle, walk, and swim. They are often good at sports. They have good fine-motor skills. They like to take things apart and put them back together. They enjoy working with their fingers.

Here are some ways to strengthen your body movement intelligence:

- Take a walk while discussing a story or gathering ideas for a story.
- Walk around the room while reading and memorizing facts and strategies.
- Use the whole arm (extended without bending the elbow) to write letters and words in the air.
- Write in a different location and use different kinds of tools to write, such as a computer, blackboard, or large piece of paper.
- Write on a mirror with lipstick or soap.

1.3.3 Musical Learners

People who have a strong musical intelligence like the rhythm and sound of language. They like poems, songs, and jingles. They enjoy humming or singing along with music.

Here are some ways to strengthen your musical intelligence:

- Sing in the shower or whilst driving your car or anywhere!
- Go to concerts or musicals.
- Join a choir.
- Learn to write poetry.
- Learn to play a musical instrument.
- Spend thirty minutes a week listening to an unfamiliar style of music for you (e.g., jazz, country & western, classical, folk, heavy rock, house music, etc.).

- Put on background music whilst studying, cooking, dressing, or eating.

- Listen for naturally occurring melodies or rhythms in such phenomena as footsteps, birdsong, and even washing machines!

- Make up a jingle, rap, or rhyme of key things you want to remember.

- Use a familiar tune, song, or rap beat to teach spelling rules or to remember words in a series for a test.

- If you have difficulty memorizing a fact, associate it with music you enjoy.

1.3.4 Interpersonal Learners or Social Intelligence

People who have a strong social intelligence like to develop ideas and learn from other people. They like to talk. They have good social skills.

Here are some ways to strengthen your social or interpersonal intelligence:

- Get organized! Use a time management system to make sure you keep in touch regularly with your network of friends.

- Join a volunteer or service-oriented group.

- Start a hobby that involves you having to go to a regular meeting of like-minded people.

- Join a charitable activity.

- Spend 15 minutes each day practicing active listening with a close friend.

- Throw a party and invite people you don't know very well.
- Take a leadership role — at school or in the community.
- Participate in workshops or seminars in interpersonal and communication skills.
- Have more frequent family meetings.
- Strike up conversation with people in public places.
- Find several pen friends from different cultures and parts of the world.
- Offer to tutor other people on an informal basis in an area in which you have expertise.
- Study the lives of well-known, socially competent people and decide what you want to "model" from them.
- Make a list of all the people that you love and make sure you tell them all this month.

1.3.5 Introvert or Intrapersonal Learners

Those with intrapersonal intelligence have the ability to be reflective and access their inner feelings. Intrapersonal learners are able to learn from past events because they can analyze and interpret these events.

Here are some ways to strengthen your intrapersonal intelligence:

- Learn to meditate or just set aside quiet time alone to think.
- Study philosophy—especially the different schools of thought from different cultures.
- Find a counsellor or therapist and explore yourself.

- Create your own personal ritual that makes you feel good.

- Read self-help books and listen to tapes.

- Establish a quiet place in your home for reflection.

- Develop an interest or hobby that sets you apart from the crowd.

- Make a personal development plan.

- Set short and long-term goals for yourself and then follow through on them.

- Attend a course designed to help you explore yourself and your potential.

- Keep a daily journal for recording your thoughts, dreams, goals, feelings, and memories.

- Study the biographies of great individuals with powerful personalities who made a real impact on the world.

- Do something to spoil yourself at least once a day.

- Keep a mirror handy and notice how your face changes depending on what kind of mood you're in.

- Spend time with people who have a strong and healthy sense of self.

- Engage in daily self-esteem enhancing behaviors—such as listing your successes, positive self-talk, and so on.

- Write your own autobiography.

1.3.6 Logical Learners

Logical learners are able to calculate and work out relationships and connections between items. They enjoy mental challenges and seeking out solutions to logical, abstract, and mathematical problems. They also have good deductive reasoning skills. On a lesser scale, they may simply excel at games involving skill and strategy, such as chess or computer battle games.

Logical-mathematical intelligence may be defined as the ability to appreciate and calculate the effect of actions upon objects or ideas and the relationships among them. Logical learners can apply inductive and deductive reasoning skills to provide solutions and to overcome complex mathematical and logical challenges as well as critical and creative problems.

People who are strong in the logic intelligence enjoy exploring how things are related. They like to understand how things work. They like mathematical concepts. They are good at critical thinking.

Here are some ways to strengthen your logical-mathematical intelligence:

- Play logical/mathematical games with friends and family.
- Work on logic puzzles and brain teasers.
- Learn basic computer programming.
- Take a course in basic
- math or science.
- Read the business section of the newspaper and look up unfamiliar economic or financial concepts.
- Visit a science museum.

- Record yourself talking out loud about how to solve logical or mathematical problems.
- Purchase a telescope and a microscope and discover the world around you.

1.3.7 Language Learners

Language learners have the ability to write and/or speak fluently, while utilizing a broad vocabulary to express the precise meaning of what they wish to convey. They can speak almost melodically with changing intonations and rhythms of sound to express feelings.

Individuals with linguistic intelligence will have one or more of the following skills:

- Rhetorical Skills: The ability to use language as a tool for persuasion and negotiation.
- Literature Skills: The ability to choose words well when writing, in order to generate the right emotional tone in letters, poems, stories, academic or business reports, etc.
- A good verbal memory for what is read, spoken, or written.

The advantages of developing one's linguistic intelligence are many. We use language to explain, persuade, sell, argue, speak publicly, describe, and write. It is a skill used extensively by lawyers, politicians, and businessmen.

The following is a list of activities that have been designed to help practice linguistic intelligence. Have a look through each item and perhaps try a few activities that you feel may help improve an area in which you consider yourself to be weak.

- Join a book club.

- Attend a workshop on writing through a local college.
- Record yourself speaking and listen to the playback to see what you can improve.
- Join a speaker's club.
- Subscribe to a high-quality newspaper with substance.
- Listen and watch recordings of famous orators, e.g., Martin Luther King, Winston Churchill, and Nelson Mandela.
- Record yourself talking out loud about how to solve a logic or science problem.
- Find opportunities to tell stories to children (and adults).
- Attend a speed-reading seminar.
- Teach an illiterate person to read through a voluntary group or charity.
- Borrow or buy audio recordings of great literature (e.g., Shakespeare, Dickens, or Tolstoy) and listen to them during your free time.

1.4 Setting a Goal for Yourself

> What we find is that if you have a goal that is very, very far out, and you approach it in little steps, you start to get there faster. Your mind opens up to the possibilities.
> —Mae Carol Jemison, First African-American woman astronaut

The first thing a student needs to have is a goal. We all seek success, and we know that nothing ever comes easy. In order to achieve success we spend our lives chasing it. We first need to define our goals. Once the goal setting is done, it's time to start thinking about how to accomplish those goals. Here are many by-products of seeking success: discipline, time management, patience, social skills, networking, and understanding how to earn your success.

Becoming a superstar student takes more than academic performance. It takes other skills, which will help you to be successful in life after school too.

During my first ten years of studying at university, I realized how important it is to set goals in every aspect of life—both personal and professional. Setting clear and measurable goals can help you to understand what steps are needed to cross the finish line.

Here are some types of goals to consider:

- Academic grades
- Social life
- Sports and exercise
- Family
- Overcoming stress
- Long-term goals
- Happiness

1.4.1 Academic Grades

When you set yourself this goal, you have to ask yourself the following questions:

1. What profession do I want to choose?

2. What grades do I require for the targeted profession?
3. What is the admission requirement for a particular university or college?

1.4.2 Social Life

While seeking to become a superstar student, you meet and interact with people on the path to your goal. In a later section I will discuss how your selection of friends can influence the outcome of your goal.

It is important that you select similar-minded people to have around you so you don't have to waste energy fighting to be accepted in groups where you don't belong.

1.4.3 Sports and Exercise

Why should students exercise?

Not only is exercise good for your overall health and fitness, it also boosts your mental wellbeing. Exercise will help keep you calm during exams. You'll feel more energized and refreshed and that will help you perform better in your studies.

Also, regular physical activity will help to keep you at a healthy weight and lower your risk of major illnesses.

Keeping active doesn't require a lot of time and effort.

You don't need to make a special trip to a sports center to reach your weekly quota of exercise. There are easy ways to get some exercise into your daily routine:

- Walk to your lectures instead of taking the bus.
- Take the stairs rather than the elevator.

- If you have a bike, ride it to class or go for a bike ride with friends.

- Rent or buy an exercise DVD. share the cost (and the fun) with your friends.

- Go for a jog with friends before going to college or in between classes.

- At lunchtime or weekends, kick a football around with your friends in the park.

1.4.4 Family

In the course of your journey to become a successful student, you will need the support of your family. Research indicates that it is the attitude towards education within the family unit that really matters.

1.4.5 Overcoming Stress

As a student, you might find that every spare minute seems to be filled with worry and the pressure of having to achieve something and plan for your future. Instead of relaxing during the holidays, you're planning an internship to add to your CV or working to earn some much needed extra cash.

If you're not careful, working too hard and worrying too much can lead to "burnout".

It might not seem like it when you're feeling down, but living a less stressful life is possible.

In the second key you will learn how to deal with stress in an effective way.

1.4.6 Long-term Goals

Having long-term goals allows you to see beyond today's work and keep your motivation high, especially when you are faced with tedious, but necessary everyday school tasks. Long-term goals cannot be achieved overnight. They may last anywhere from one year to a few decades.

There is a big difference between saying, "Someday I will be an accomplished Engineer," and "By 2018, I will get my Master's Degree in Mechanical Engineering at M.I.T." The first statement is a dream that has nothing to do with reality. The second statement is a long-term goal that combines a dream to become an accomplished Engineer and a plan on how to get there. When setting long term goals, make sure that they are specific, measurable, attainable, realistic and timely.

1.4.7 Happiness

As a student, if you want to be happy you need to understand that you can be happy. Many people make the mistake of believing that they don't deserve happiness and accept their unhappy state as their fate. It is important to know that happiness, like anything else in life, needs to be cherished.

I follow these steps to create happiness in my life:

- Understand what it is that will make you happy. Do not worry about whether or not your desires are comparable to those of your fellow students. We will discuss this further in the friends and competition section.

- Make a plan for attaining the goals that you believe will make you happy. Your mood will very likely improve as you pursue your goals.

- Surround yourself with positive people.

- When you fail at something, try to figure out a solution instead of feeling ashamed. Truly happy people don't allow failure to affect their mood because they know that with a strong mind they can turn the circumstances back to their advantage.

- Take a few minutes each day to think about the things that make you happy. These few minutes will give you the opportunity to focus on the positive things in your life.

- Be nice to yourself. Treat yourself to delicious food or take a long, relaxing bath. You will be subconsciously putting yourself in a better mood.

- Find a way to make light of a situation that would otherwise make you unhappy.

- Exercise. As mentioned before, exercise has been known to release endorphins that give you a feeling of happiness.

Tell yourself each day that you deserve to be happy and remind yourself what steps you will take to achieve the happiness you desire.

1.5 How Great Minds Viewed Intelligence

One of my main goals in this book is to show you that you don't need to be a super math genius to succeed in school and life. With the right approach toward day-to-day life tasks, you can take control of your destiny and achieve high standards in academic life and beyond. I have gathered some of the great minds' observations on intelligence. These different views show you there are many ways to observe the world and find your own way toward success. You can be a successful student with your own unique intelligence. So get started!

Let's take a look at how some great minds see intelligence:

> THE TRUE SIGN OF INTELLIGENCE IS NOT KNOWLEDGE BUT IMAGINATION.
> —ALBERT EINSTEIN (1879 – 1955), THEORETICAL PHYSICIST

> THE INTELLIGENT MAN IS ONE WHO HAS SUCCESSFULLY FULFILLED MANY ACCOMPLISHMENTS AND IS YET WILLING TO LEARN MORE.
> —ED PARKER. EDMUND KEALOHA ("ED") PARKER (1931 – 1990) WAS AN AMERICAN MARTIAL ARTIST, PROMOTER, TEACHER, AND AUTHOR. HE HELPED BRUCE LEE GAIN NATIONAL ATTENTION BY INTRODUCING HIM AT HIS INTERNATIONAL KARATE CHAMPIONSHIPS.

> CONTINUOUS EFFORT—NOT STRENGTH OR INTELLIGENCE—IS THE KEY TO UNLOCKING OUR POTENTIAL.
> —WINSTON CHURCHILL (1874 – 1965), PRIME MINISTER OF THE UNITED KINGDOM DURING WWII.

> I KNOW THAT I AM INTELLIGENT, BECAUSE I KNOW THAT I KNOW NOTHING.
> SOCRATES (469 – 399 BC), GREEK PHILOSOPHER.

> INTELLIGENCE IS THE ABILITY TO TAKE IN INFORMATION FROM THE WORLD AND TO FIND PATTERNS IN THAT INFORMATION THAT ALLOW YOU TO ORGANIZE YOUR PERCEPTIONS AND UNDERSTAND THE EXTERNAL WORLD.
> —BRIAN GREENE, BORN FEBRUARY 9, 1963, IS AN AMERICAN THEORETICAL PHYSICIST WHO IS FANTASTIC AT PRESENTING COMPLEX PHYSICS CONCEPTS IN A SIMPLE AND ENJOYABLE WAY.

....

1.6 A Lesson from My Learning Style

When I started to prepare for admission to university, the overwhelming feeling of being consumed by information and work prevented me from enjoying that stage of life. When you are thrown into the unknown, it is hard to navigate your way through a jungle of information. I soon found I learned best when studying in a team or study group because there was always someone who had an idea how to solve or think through an assignment.

My hope for this book is that it provides you with some useful tools, and that you know that you are not alone.

If I knew then, what I know now, my university life would have been more enjoyable. It is important to keep the big picture in mind instead of constantly worrying about the unknowns of academic life.

EXERCISES

Exercise 1: *List the top ten role models in your life who inspire you:*

1 ....

2 ....

3 ....

4 ....

5 ....

6 ....

7 ....

8 ....

9 ....

10 ....

Exercise 2: *Make a list of your goals in life:*

1 ....

2 ....

3 ....

4 ....

5 ....

6 ....

7 ....

8 ....

9 ....

10 ....

Exercise 3: *Do some Internet research to find out what kind of learner you are and list your scores in the different learning styles:*

1 ....

2 ....

3 ....

4 ....

5 ....

6 ....

7 ....

8 ....

9 ....

10 ....

Second Key:
Learn to Cope with Stress

The greatest weapon against stress is our ability to choose one thought over another.
—William James (1842 – 1910), philosopher.

Topics in this section:

- What Is Your Personal Image?
- Media Influence
- Academic Pressure
- Steps to Reduce Your Stress
- How Great Minds Viewed Stress

Introduction

Stress is defined as a state of mental or emotional strain or tension resulting from adverse or very demanding circumstances. Stress is a problem because most students do not know how to handle it.

In your journey to become a successful student you need to learn to deal with it because your mental and physical performance depends on it.

I know from my own experience that there are many sources of stress, but as a student I mostly faced the ones covered in the following sections.

2.1 What Is Your Personal Image?

> I pay no attention whatever to anybody's praise or blame. I simply follow my own feelings.
> —Wolfgang Amadeus Mozart (1756 – 1791), composer.

A student's social well-being depends largely upon his or her perception of his or her personal image and identity. Some students may feel insecure about appearance and body image while comparing themselves to peers. They feel that they must compete with others to measure up athletically, musically, scholastically, or in popularity. When students are rejected from a group, they may feel stress from a deep sense of inadequacy that takes over their lives. Sometimes students may spend a great amount of time concentrating on the aspects of others, hindering their own attempts to find out who they really are.

Self-perception theory: William James was an American philosopher and psychologist who was one of the leading thinkers of the late nineteenth century in America. He proposed the theory of self. That is to say: If you want to be confident act as confident person.

> NO ONE CAN MAKE YOU FEEL INFERIOR WITHOUT YOUR CONSENT.
> —ANNA ELEANOR ROOSEVELT (1884 – 1962), AMERICAN POLITICIAN.

In the eighties, when I was a student at high school, I wore glasses that were thick and bulky, and suffered from a self-image crisis. I had this nagging idea that I looked inadequate with my bulky glasses. Now I realize that that could have been a positive image because I wanted to be an engineer, so having glasses was self-assurance that I would study a lot and look smart.

What is the lesson for you? You can control your self-image as long as you act on it. Eventually the image you are seeking becomes reality. Let's take a look at a quote from Professor Isaac Asimov. Asimov was a scientist, and one of the most prolific science fiction writers of all time with more than 500 books to his credit.

> AND ABOVE ALL THINGS NEVER THINK THAT YOU'RE NOT GOOD ENOUGH YOURSELF. A MAN SHOULD NEVER THINK THAT. MY BELIEF IS THAT IN LIFE PEOPLE WILL TAKE YOU AT YOUR OWN RECKONING.
> —ISAAC ASIMOV (1920 – 1992), SCIENTIST AND SCIENCE FICTION WRITER.

You will think better and make better decisions if you have peace of mind. The one thing that determines your look is your attitude.

Exercise

- Find honest friends around you, and ask them to describe how they see you.
- Take note of their observations and sit alone and ask yourself if these observations are compatible with your self-image and bring you peace of mind.

Here are some ways to work on your self-esteem and enhance your personal image:

- Determine the realistic limitations of your behavior and abilities.
- Don't let anyone take your pride away.
- Master one sport within your abilities.
- Exercise humility.
- Volunteer at a charity.
- Pursue a noble activity that brings out the best in you.
- Strengthen your skills in the areas that come easiest.

- Seek hobbies that can be carried on in your life beyond school—like playing golf or painting.

2.2 Media Influence

Media messages exert powerful influences upon students. "Media" consists of all electronic and print forms used for sharing information. The most common types in the lives of students are the Internet, TV, and music. Virtually everyone is influenced by some kind of media on a daily basis. It bombards us with some truth, some half-truths, and some lies. Students have very little influence on the media because it is controlled by adults. However students get blamed for the way the media influences them.

What to do with media influence? Since we can become a product of our environment we can choose the type of media from which we get our information.

Exercise

- List the media sources you are connected to and ask yourself if they provide you with the type of information and influence that brings you peace of mind.
- Are the media sources you are watching compatible with your values? Do you copy behaviors from media sources that are not yours?

Here are some suggestions on how to get the best out of the media:

- Be aware of the types of medias to which you are exposed.
- Watch movies that make you feel good.

- Teach yourself the art of critical thinking. Use this skill to ask yourself what the motivation is behind everything you receive from the Internet, TV, and/or other media.

2.3 Academic Pressure

School stress is serious business. Students are being pushed to perform and make big academic progress. Some students are terrified of failing the standardized tests now emphasized heavily during the school year. This school stress takes a toll on many students. Having to deal with so many things at this stage of your life can be a painful process, but getting ahead and growth has a cost and the learning process is not always easy.

2.3.1 Managing Time

Time stays long enough for anyone who will use it.

—Leonardo da Vinci (1452 – 1519), scientist, inventor, and artist.

These days, time seems to be at a premium. We have devices that keep us constantly connected with work, friends and family, and sometimes even complete strangers. As a result, it's easy to get distracted. You have a lot to accomplish. I'll show you a great way to do just that!

Here is a simple time management system to follow:

1. Prepare yourself first by taking 30 minutes of your time to fix yourself something to eat and relax.

2. Write down your weekly tasks in order of priority. Assign realistic priorities to each task, for example:
Priority 1: Due today by 6pm
Priority 2: Due tomorrow by 6pm

Priority 3: Due by the end of the week
Priority 4: Due during next week

3. Scientifically, it is known that 45 minutes of work followed by a 10-minute rest is the best routine for the average person who is studying. Turn off your phone and television. Kick out your friends and siblings. Focus every atom of attention you have on the task at hand. You can check your messages during your short break.

4. Keep track of your progress. Cross things off the list as they are completed. You'll feel more relieved and relaxed just by getting through the daily tasks. Not only will you be getting things done, finishing tasks will give you a sense of accomplishment and increase your motivation.

2.3.2 Organize Yourself

The idea of doing homework is to practice so new information gets established in the brain. I would use the analogy of a nail and hammer. The more you hit the nail into the wall the deeper it gets inside. The information you learn in school is the same.

1. Organize information from the first day in school. Get a folder for each subject and divide it into sections for each class' notes, homework, and tests. Select a different color for each subject.

2. Label the folder with your name and subject.

3. Get a planner. Planners can help keep you in the right direction and save you valuable time. Write down homework, tests, and club meetings before you go home.

2.3.3 Create a Good Studying Environment

Here are some steps for creating your study environment:

1. Research shows that most students study best in a quiet environment. Turn off your phone. Try to pull out the plug for the TV, so even if you try, it won't work. If you want music, play something that has no words. You can choose soft music that fits your taste or mood and cultural background. Classical music, such as Mozart, is very helpful and enables you to retain information faster.

2. Be alert. Try to study at a desk. Soft couches and beds can be comfortable, but you'll probably end up getting sleepy.

3. Don't dim the lights. That will just increase the risk of falling asleep. Turn on as many lights as possible. Not only will you be less likely to fall asleep, but you can see everything more clearly with proper lighting.

4. I found studying in a cooler room prevented me from falling asleep. Adjust the working temperature. If your study place is too warm, you might become sleepy. Select a temperature at which your mind and body function best.

5. It is very important to have uninterrupted study time. You may have to hang a "DO NOT DISTURB" sign on the door or take the phone off the hook.

2.3.4 Exam Fever

Taking control of your fear is easier said than done. There are many techniques that can help you get into a mental state of relaxation. However, it may take time and trial and error to reach the point where you can control your fear when you are sitting down for an exam. The following relaxation techniques will help you:

- Relax. You are in control. Take slow, deep breaths.

- Don't think about the fear. Pause. Think about the next step and keep on task, step by step.

- Use positive reinforcement for yourself. Acknowledge that you are doing your best.

Think about any success you had in the past, no matter how small, and reinforce your positive thoughts.

It is always a challenge to go through an exam. There are many factors influencing exam performance, so you cannot judge your intelligence based on one exam. If you are nervous, tired, overexcited, and/or overconfident when taking a test, it may ruin your performance even if you know the subject. I will now give you my own tips, based on my 10 years of experience, on how to deal with each one of these factors.

The majority of people do experience nervousness. To overcome this, you must mentally strengthen yourself. This can be done by preparation. I recommend the following steps:

Before the test:

- Approach the exam with confidence: Use whatever strategies you can to personalize success—visualization, logic, talking to yourself, practice, teamwork.

- Be prepared: Learn your material thoroughly and organize what materials you will need for the test. Use a checklist for the things you must have and tick each item as you check it.

At the location:

- Choose a comfortable location—with good lighting and minimal distractions—for taking the test.

- Strive for a relaxed state of concentration.

- Avoid speaking with any fellow students who have not prepared, who express negativity, or who will distract your preparation.

- Allow yourself plenty of time.

Things you need to do before the test and still get there a little early:

- Get a good night's sleep the night before the exam.

- Don't go to the exam with an empty stomach. Fresh fruits and vegetables are often recommended to reduce stress.

During the test:

- Read the directions carefully.

- Budget your test taking time.

- Change positions to help you relax.

- If you go blank, skip the question and continue to the next question. Come back when you have finished answering the questions that are easy for you.

- If you're taking an essay test and you go blank on the whole test, pick a question and start writing. It may trigger the answer in your mind.

- Don't panic when students start handing in their papers. There's no reward for finishing first.

After the test:

- List what worked and hold onto these strategies. It does not matter how small the items are: They are building blocks to success.

- List what did not work for improvement.

- Celebrate that you are on the road to overcoming this obstacle.

2.4 Steps to Reduce Your Stress

If you're not careful, working too hard and worrying too much can lead to "burnout".

It might not seem like it when you're feeling down, but living a less stressful life is possible. When I was a student, these easy ways helped me to beat stress effectively:

- Exercise: I did mention before the easy ways to get your exercise. Doing a sport at least once a week is a good way to reduce stress. It helps your body produce endorphins, which make you feel good. Even 30-minute daily walks can help reduce stress levels. Even if you don't feel like it at the time, you will feel the benefits afterwards.

- Meditation: It might sound simple, but sitting quietly for 10 minutes a day can really help with stress levels. If you've never tried meditation before, it's worth a go.

- Good breathing techniques can put you in a more relaxed state as they send oxygen surging through your bloodstream, helping to calm you down and beat the stress.

- Take breaks regularly: How about taking the weekend off to relax? Make time for fun and for yourself even if this means that you have to schedule time away from your work. You'll hopefully come back to your work feeling fresh. Short breaks between working can help you switch off, but longer breaks are important too.

- Sleep is always the best medicine, and some people find that small 20-minute naps can help increase productivity. As students, we tend to spend too much time on social media sites and answering emails, texts, and phone calls. Socializing is fun—but too much of it, and too much computer time, can lead to more stress. Failing to switch off from work because of your electronic gadgets will only make you more stressed.

- See the positive side: If you missed a deadline, try to appreciate what you learned from this mistake. Now you know how to plan ahead. Things might seem bad, but if you try, there is usually something positive to be learned.

- Laugh: They say that laughter is the best medicine, and it's really true. Laughing out loud increases oxygen and blood flow, which automatically reduces stress. Not taking life too seriously can help everyone live a better and easier life.

2.4.1 Diet

Diet is the intake of food considered in relation to the body's dietary needs. Good nutrition combined with regular physical activity is a cornerstone of good health. Poor nutrition can lead to reduced immunity, increased susceptibility to disease, impaired physical and mental development, and reduced productivity at school.

- Eating fresh ingredients and lots of fruit is really important. Juices filled with vitamin C, such as orange and grapefruit juice, are said to be good for your immune system.

These foods really helped me when I was student:Nuts and seeds. Nuts and seeds are a rich source of Omega 3 and Omega 6 essential fatty acids, which help reduce stress. Walnuts: Look at one. It is like a brain. Walnuts are a nutrient-dense food that earned one of the first approved qualified health claims by the U.S. Food and Drug Administration as a "whole food". Unique among nuts, walnuts contain the highest amount of alpha-linolenic acid (ALA), the plant-based Omega-3 essential fatty acid. I realized that on stressful days walnuts helped me to get through the day with less friction. Have a handful each day. Almonds: Make you feel energetic. Almonds are an excellent source of vitamin E, magnesium, and manganese, and a good source of fibre, copper, and phosphorous. When I was a student, I carried a small bag with this magical food in my backpack and enjoyed it when I felt tired. I tell you I got a turbo boost. Oranges and apples: These have high vitamin C content. If you are allergic to nuts eat these fruits. They can help you to feel fresh, and their high vitamin C content will fight off the stress.

2.4.2 The Power of Music

> Music is the one incorporeal entrance into the higher world of knowledge which comprehends mankind, but which mankind cannot comprehend.
> —Ludwig van Beethoven (1770 – 1827), composer.

....

My personal experience confirms that music can have a deep effect on both the emotions and the body. You can choose a soft music that fits your taste or mood and your cultural background. Classical music can make you feel more alert and help you to concentrate better. Upbeat music can make you feel more optimistic and positive about life. A slower tempo can quiet your mind and relax your muscles, making you feel relaxed while releasing the stress of the day. Music is effective for relaxation and stress management.

I recommend two musical masterpieces:

- *Eine kleine Nachtmusik* by Wolfgang Amadeus Mozart (1756 – 1791)

- *Air on the G String* by Johann Sebastian Bach (1685 – 1750)

2.4.3 The Power of Water

> Water is the driving force of all nature.
> —Leonardo da Vinci (1452 – 1519), scientist, inventor, and artist.

Water is a great "anxiety quencher". When the body is dehydrated, it can actually induce anxiety and nervousness. When we are dehydrated, our cells feel it at the molecular level. Taking a warm bath with an herbal supplement can do wonders for the body and soul. Sounds like a cliché, but the hot water will literally ease muscle tension.

Studies link depression to dehydration because 85% of brain tissue is water. Dehydration causes energy generation in the brain to decrease, so a lack of water can be the culprit in some mood disorders. Therefore, in order to reduce your stress try to keep a glass of water at your desk or carry a sports bottle and sip from it regularly.

2.4.4 The Power of Writing Your Thoughts

As the body discharges waste, our minds need to discharge those annoying thoughts that somehow we cannot get rid off.

One technique that I used when I was a student was flushing the garbage thoughts down the toilet. This is simply done by writing down all those things that cross your mind about a situation or a person. This is how you do it:

- Get a white piece of paper.

- Go to a quiet place.

- Write down all the bothering thoughts.

- Go to the washroom and tear the paper into small pieces.

- Throw it in the toilet and flush.

I guarantee it. You will feel much better. For practical purposes, make sure you tear up the paper into small enough pieces so that they don't block the toilet!

2.5 How Great Minds Viewed Stress

> The mind ought sometimes to be diverted that it may return to better thinking.
> —Phaedrus (444 BC – 393 BC), Athenian aristocrat.

Thomas Alva Edison (1847 – 1931) was one of the greatest inventors of all time. I have read his biography many times, and he dealt with stress by "switching his thinking". Every time he got stressed with a project, he switched his mind to a fresh new activity. In this way he replaced the stressful thoughts with fresh thoughts and focused on being productive in different work. Does this work? The proof is there: He had 1093 patents to his credit.

Hans Selye (1907 – 1982) was a pioneering Austrian-Canadian endocrinologist of Hungarian origin. He conducted much important scientific work on stress. He said:

- "Adopting the right attitude can convert a negative stress into a positive one."

- "Man should not try to avoid stress any more than he would shun food, love, or exercise."
- "It is not stress that kills us, it is our reaction to it."

Exercises

Exercise 1: *Each week, write down the thoughts that are bothering you:*

1 ....
2 ....
3 ....
4 ....
5 ....
6 ....
7 ....
8 ....
9 ....
10 ....

Exercise 2: *Write down a list of sports activities that you are able to do:*

1 ....
2 ....
3 ....

4 ....
5 ....
6 ....
7 ....
8 ....
9 ....
10 ....

Exercise 3: *Write down a list of your top ten favorite comedies, and watch them when you feel down:*

1 ....
2 ....
3 ....
4 ....
5 ....
6 ....
7 ....
8 ....
9 ....
10 ....

Third Key:
Friends and Competition

Be courteous to all, but intimate with few, and let those few be well tried before you give them your confidence.
—George Washington, first President of the United States. (1789–1797)

Topics in this section:

- Why Is It Important Who You Befriend?
- Communication Skills.
- How to Choose a Friend.
- My Personal Experience.
- How Great Minds Viewed Friendship.
- Recommended Books and Magazines.

Introduction

Once a wise man told me that the people you associate with and the books you read will become your future five years from now. In my own experience, that is very true. It is said that we are products of our environment. So why not choose the environment?

One way to find out if your friends are having a positive effect on you is to measure your mood after you've been with them. Do you leave feeling strengthened and happy? If so, chances are your friends are a good influence on your mind and physique.

3.1 Why Is It Important Who You Befriend?

In the journey of life, we meet people with different values and standards. When you start school or college, there will be many opportunities to meet people. You can't expect that everybody you meet will become your friend. In your career as a student, communication skills are important tools in your tool box. One application is that they will help you to make yourself known to your peers and find a friend. I like to use the analogy of a tool box when studying at school or college. Each subject you are learning will be added to your tool box, and by the end of your school years, you will have a toolbox for the future challenges you will face. The more skills and knowledge you acquire, the more complete your tool box becomes.

3.2 Communication Skills

Communication is critical to social situations, school, family, and the workplace. Learning communication skills allows you to avoid conflict. Here are some steps to develop these crucial skills that will help you in your personal and professional life:

1. Think before you speak. Allow yourself a pause to consider how your words could be perceived and to prevent yourself from making hasty comments.

2. Consider the other person's viewpoint. For example, you might say: "I see how your friend's behavior could be annoying to you."

3. Be culturally aware. Consider cultural differences, and try to act in a sensitive way without being asked. It will be hard to know the meaning of many behaviors or gestures unless you study them closely.

4. Be discrete. Correct someone in private when you see an obvious mistake.

5. Be gracious even when you're irritated. Keep your cool and speak kindly and sincerely. Assume the best.

6. Deflect negative comments. Say something that shows you don't have all the information, for example: "I've never met Mike, so I wouldn't have a clue about his drinking habits." Another option is to say nothing.

7. Think of positive things to say. Make a comment to one of your teachers about something you find interesting or a new project that you like to do.

3.3 How to Choose a Friend

When I was looking for friends, I always asked myself the following questions:

- Do they accept me for my values?
- How do I keep my mind open? What can I learn from a different culture?

When looking for a friend, try to use my whole picture approach. Will your friend distract or discourage you from your goal? Ask yourself, does he or she:

- Blather?
- Ask you to do illegal activities?
- Make you harm yourself or people around you? Act carelessly with the environment and/or animals?

If the answer is "yes" to any of these, then stand up for yourself and say "no".

You can find like-minded friends by following these steps:

- Do you have a preferred hobby, sport, or interest? If you do, there's a good chance that there are people out there who share your interest.

- Look for an online forum where people are either interested in meeting new people or people share similar interests.

- Don't fight for acceptance. Let me make it easy for you: Your friends either accept you for who you are or you find someone else who appreciates the way you look, feel, and live.

3.4 My Personal Experience

My quest for science led me to hit the road alone at the early age of 13. When I left my home country, I was so occupied with a sense of adventure that I did not think about the many possible dangers until they occurred. I will write a book about my encounters in this quest for science.

When I left Germany in 1986 and took a train to Denmark, I was received by the Danish Red Cross. I resided in a small village called Marslev. I was given a room and some cooking utensils.

I initially thought that I would be the only child in this camp because no other child would be crazy enough to come alone to this country. Then I met a young, skinny boy walking around in the village. His name was Carl. I invited him to my room for a tea, and we started our friendship.

Carl had a lot of anger in him and didn't want to sit down and study Danish with me. We were being ridiculed a lot by some Danish kids in the village, but since we could not respond, we just had to take it. I knew that if we learned the slang, we could throw some of the nasty words back at them. However, it required that we sit down and learn the language.

When I think back to those days, I realize that Carl and I did not share the same goal. I wanted to learn Danish and dig in those dusty dictionaries for vocabulary while Carl wanted to take a tour bus to the German border and buy beer.

I am presenting you my experience to make the point about shared interests.

The table below shows my and Carl's interests and plans:

Carl	Mehdi
• Drinking beer	• Learning Danish
• Hanging around the mall	• Reading scientific magazine
• Shopping over the budget	• Walking in nature and watching birds
• Had no plans for the future	• Wanted to be an engineer

I am not saying we did not have fun. We just did not share the same interests or have common values. Your friends don't need to be perfect (because none of us are), but they should encourage you.

Because Carl was constantly buying fancy cologne, he borrowed money. It reached a stage that because of his carelessness, he did not pay his debt to me and we parted ways.

After a few months, the Danish Red Cross realized that we needed to go in the care of a Danish family. I did not see Carl again. I did hear that he got involved in illegal substance trading and got into trouble.

I am not saying to be a robot. I am saying have fun without harming yourself and others.

3.5 How Great Mind Viewed Friendship

We can learn from how great minds viewed friendship.

> *Lots of people want to ride with you in the limo, but what you want is someone who will take the bus with you when the limo breaks down.*
> —Oprah Winfrey, talk show host, actress, producer, and philanthropist.

> *Fine manners need the support of fine manners in others. It is one of the blessings of old friends that you can afford to be stupid with them.*
> —Ralph Waldo Emerson (1803 – 1882) was an American essayist, lecturer, and poet, who led a literary and philosophical movement of the mid-19th century.

> *A friend is one who knows you and loves you just the same.*
> —Elbert Green Hubbard (1856 – 1915) was an American writer, publisher, artist, and philosopher.

> *One of the most beautiful qualities of true friendship is to understand and to be understood.*
> —Lucius Annaeus Seneca (4 BC — AD 65) was a Roman philosopher.

> *Friendship is a single soul dwelling in two bodies.*
> —Aristotle (384 BC – 322 BC) was a Greek philosopher and a scientist. This true genius had a sea of accomplishments. One of his major contributions was the establishment of scientific methods such as logic. He contributed immensely in many fields of human knowledge.

> *I have friends in overalls whose friendship I would not swap for the favor of the kings of the world.*
> —Thomas A. Edison (1847 – 1931) was an American inventor with more than a thousand patents. His inventions revolutionized many industries world-wide. Just his invention of the electric light bulb and an electricity distribution system improved the life of humanity.

3.6 Recommended Books and Magazines

During my journey in Europe and all those lonely nights at the train station or the Red Cross camp, I had a science magazine with me. Because of my language barrier and lack of friends, books and magazines were a great comfort. I had the following items with me no matter where I went:

- *Asimov's Guide to Science,* 1984.

- *Scientist Magazine,* 1984.

In the course of all my years at school and university, I had the following subscriptions:

- *Illustrated Science (Danish Science Magazine)*

- *Scientific American*

- *Newsweek*

- *Focus* (British Science Magazine)

I would recommend scanning through the magazine rack at your local news outlet and seeing what is of interest to read. The idea is to expand your reading spectrum and learn new vocabulary and knowledge. I chose science magazines because that is what I enjoy. You could read entertainment, world news, finance, nature, or sports magazines. Once you get into the habit of reading, your mind switches to a rest mode, and after that, you return to your school reading in a more energized manner.

Recommended reading from Isaac Asimov:

How Did We Find Out About Atoms?

The Planet That Wasn't

The Bicentennial Man and Other Stories

Alpha Centauri, the Nearest Star

How Did We Find Out About Outer Space?

EXERCISES

Exercise 1: *List the top ten qualities you seek in a friendship:*

1 ....

2 ....

3 ....

4 ....

5 ....

6 ....

7 ....

8 ....

9 ....

10 ....

Exercise 2: *List the top ten places where you can socialize and find friends with common interests:*

1 ....

2 ....
3 ....
4 ....
5 ....
6 ....
7 ....
8 ....
9 ....
10 ....

Exercise 3: *Make a list of the top ten books that energize you, and read one when you feel lonely:*

1 ....
2 ....
3 ....
4 ....
5 ....
6 ....
7 ....
8 ....
9 ....
10 ....

Fourth Key: Don't Give Up

> Our greatest weakness lies in giving up. The most certain way to succeed is always to try just one more time.
> —Thomas A. Edison (1847 – 1931), inventor.

Topics in this section:

- Why You Need Persistence
- How to Develop Your Persistence

- Inspiration from Nature
- How Great Minds Viewed Success
- My Experience

Introduction

When we are faced with challenges in our life, we tend to find the easy way out. But the easy way might not be the best way. Keeping in mind examples of people who achieved success and their techniques will not only comfort us, it will also change our lives for the better if we act on it. The aim of this secret is to show you how you can bring yourself up when you are down and how to encourage yourself to move forward when faced with challenges. We as human beings are capable of unbelievable things because of the capacity of our brains. We can learn and enhance our intelligence by looking at life's ups and downs with an educational point of view.

4.1 Why You Need Persistence

The capacity to get back up after we have been knocked down is important for us to achieve success.

Many famous and successful people had to fail over and over again to achieve their success in life. In this section, I will show you through my own personal experience how persistence can help you achieve your goals. On your journey to become a "superstar", there will be failures. It's how you deal with these failures that will determine the outcome of your journey to become a superstar student. Many students don't pursue their dreams for fear of failure, but failure is one of the biggest ways we learn and develop. Failure forces us to develop a personal quality called persistence.

One of my personal heroes and role models is Thomas Alva Edison, an American inventor and businessman. He developed many devices that greatly influenced life around the world, including the phonograph, the motion picture camera, and the light bulb.

Thomas Edison's teachers called him "stupid", and he was fired many times. He made 10,000 attempts before gaining success in the functional light bulb that we still enjoy to this day.

Another role model of mine is Morihei Ueshiba, who viewed failure as a step stone to success.

Morihei Ueshiba (1883 – 1969) was a martial artist and founder of the Japanese martial art of aikido. He famously declared:

> "Failure is the key to success ; each mistake teaches us something".

4.2 How to Develop Your Persistence

Persistence is not taught. You will need to look at examples and see that "failures" are only temporary.

The three main steps that worked for me in the face of setbacks were:

- Keep a positive mind
- Keep trying
- Keep a role model

4.2.1 Keeping a Positive Mind

I like to use the analogy of comparing positive thoughts with fuel for your vehicle. If there is no fuel in your vehicle, you won't get far.

Positive thoughts are fuel for the mind vehicle. In the face of hopelessness, the mind is out of fuel. To start your mind engine, you need to hook on a past success—any success, no matter how insignificant, small, or remote it might appear. You need to summon it. Once you have it present, the spark appears. Now like starting a fire in the "good old days", you need to blow air into it. In this case, the air is thoughts of more past successes. And with that, your fire will start.

4.2.2 Keep Trying

Now that you have your mind full of positive thoughts, you can start the drilling process. Why do you need to keep trying?

That answer is that, in every attempt, you inch yourself forward towards success.

Robert Goddard:

Robert Hutchings Goddard (1882 – 1945) was an American physicist and inventor who designed the world's first liquid-fueled rocket, which he successfully launched on March 16, 1926.

Rocket scientist Robert Goddard found his ideas bitterly rejected by his scientific colleagues on the grounds that rocket propulsion would not work in the outer space.

Michael Jordan:

He missed more than 9000 shots in his career and he said:

> "I've failed over and over and over again in my life. That is why I succeed."

4.2.3 Keep a Role Model

The idea of a role model is that it gives you comfort and support in the time of hopelessness and difficulty. Take a look at people who you admire and tell yourself:

> "What a man can do, another man can do"

In the Russian short story, The Bridge, by Nikolai Chukovski, the main character, Kostya, said those words.

I myself had Thomas Alva Edison as my role model and it helped to be inspired and helped me to remind myself that human beings are super strong if they want to be. They just need to know that our ability to overcome the adversity is hidden in each and every one of us.

4.3 Inspiration from Nature

> Look deep into nature, and then you will understand everything better.
> —Albert Einstein (1879 – 1955), theoretical physicist.

Einstein knew something when he looked at nature. He was inspired and learned by looking at nature.

I would like to bring nature to your attention to show you that persistence is a quality that animals have developed in order to survive. Through nature, we learn that we can achieve our goals through persistence. Now let's look at some examples of persistence in the animal kingdom:

The cheetah is the fastest animal on land, but only 5 out of 10 hunting attempts yield a successful result.

The African lion is the second biggest cat and the "king" of the animal kingdom. It has been observed that, in spite of hunting as a team, their hunting success rate is only 3 out of 10.

The great white shark is an apex hunter of the seas and has no natural predators. It can be more than 7 metres (23 feet) long. Yet despite this, only around 5 out of 10 hunts are successful.

Golden eagles, with their majestic look, are masters of the skies. It has been observed that typically only 3 out of 10 of their hunting attempts are successful.

Killer whales have no natural predators and hunt as a team. It has been observed that 8 out of 10 hunts are successful.

WHAT DO WE LEARN FROM THE ABOVE?
DON'T GIVE UP UNTIL YOU ARE SUCCESSFUL.

4.4 How Great Minds Viewed Success

WE CAN DO ANYTHING WE WANT TO IF WE STICK TO IT LONG ENOUGH.
—HELEN ADAMS KELLER (1880 – 1968), AUTHOR, LECTURER, AND HUMANIST.

JUST DON'T GIVE UP TRYING TO DO WHAT YOU REALLY WANT TO DO. WHERE THERE IS LOVE AND INSPIRATION,
I DON'T THINK YOU CAN GO WRONG.
—ELLA JANE FITZGERALD (1917 – 1996), JAZZ VOCALIST.

I WORKED HARD. ANYONE WHO WORKS AS HARD AS I DID CAN ACHIEVE THE SAME RESULTS.
—JOHANN SEBASTIAN BACH (1685 – 1750), COMPOSER.

> BE FAITHFUL IN SMALL THINGS BECAUSE
> IT IS IN THEM THAT YOUR STRENGTH LIES.
> —MOTHER TERESA (1910 – 1997), MISSIONARY, NOBEL PEACE
> PRIZE WINNER.

Famous people achieve success, because persistence is one of their main qualities. They don't let failure stop them. Here are some examples of failures that famous people encountered:

- Steve Jobs, at age 30, was left devastated and depressed after being unceremoniously removed from the company he started.

- Michael Jordan was cut from his high-school basketball team. He went home and cried.

- Oprah Winfrey was moved down from her position as news anchor because she "wasn't fit for television".

- Thomas Alva Edison, at the age of 19, was fired from Western Union when he spilled battery liquid on the floor.

- Albert Einstein did not gain admission to a polytechnic school in Switzerland.

- Isaac Newton failed at the family business.

- The Wright brothers suffered from depression.

- Winston Churchill failed for many years in politics before becoming the Prime Minister.

- Abraham Lincoln failed in many businesses before becoming President.

- Harry S. Truman failed at business and went bankrupt.

- Harrison Ford was at first rejected by movie producers.

- Mozart was fired from his job as a court musician in Salzburg.
- Beethoven was told by his music teacher that he was hopeless.
- Walt Disney was fired from his position as newspaper editor.
- Steven Spielberg dropped out of junior high school.
- Charlie Chaplin initially was rejected by movie producers.

4.5 My Experience

In my 10 years of experience at university, I have been through thousands of math and physics assignments. I have a lot of experience in going through the process of finding a solution. During my first three years of my bachelor degree, I learned that when I stopped looking for a solution I was usually only inches away from the answer. Here is how I did it:

1. Read the assignment.
2. Understood what was being asked.
3. Attempted to find a solution.
4. Documented all the methods leading to a possible solution.
5. When unable to find the solution, went back to read the textbook.
6. Researched to see if I could find a similar assignment.
7. Learned from the similar assignment.
8. When unable to find the solution, consulted my professor.
9. Showed all attempted methods.
10. Was presented with the solution by my professor.

What did I find out?

What I discovered was always amazing. I was inches away from a solution.

That reminds me of Thomas Alva Edison's famous quote: "Many of life's failures are people who did not realize how close they were to success when they gave up."

The process is the reward. Over the months of dealing with my failures to solve math and physics problems, I discovered that I was gaining slight improvement with each failure. My knowledge base was expanding each time I went through the ten-step process.

By the end of my second year, I noticed that not only had my mind become sharper, I also had improved the quality of my persistence. That persistency element inside helped to propel me to the next semester with more confidence and a deeper knowledge.

So the ten-step process is the golden rule you need to know in order to become successful.

Exercises

Exercise 1: *List ten adversities you overcame in your life. (These can include even the smallest triumph.)*

1 ....
2 ....
3 ....
4 ....
5 ....

6 ....

7 ....

8 ....

9 ....

10 ....

Exercise 2: *Make a list of people who can encourage, exchange ideas, or brainstorm with you.*

1 ....

2 ....

3 ....

4 ....

5 ....

6 ....

7 ....

8 ....

9 ....

10 ....

Exercise 3: *Make a list of ten inspirational quotes about persistence, and display it in front of your desk.*

1 ....

2 ....

3 ....

4 ....

5 ....

6 ....

7 ....

8 ....

9 ....

10 ....

Fifth Key:
Expand Your Learning Capacity

Knowledge is love and light and vision.
—Helen Adams Keller (1880 – 1968), author, lecturer, and humanist.

Topics in this section:

- Why You Should Expand Your Learning Capacity
- Practical Steps to Expand Your Learning Capacity
- Presentation Skills
- Teamwork Skills
- How to Understand a Concept
- Practice Self-education
- How Great Minds Viewed Learning
- My Experience

Introduction

In school, learning happens in a structured way. We associate it with the hours of 9 to 3, with orderly schedules and heavy textbooks, and with boredom and the grind. At the end of the day, we leave, glad that it's finally over. This is the school system. However, we can take charge of how we can learn. School is not the only place in which learning can occur. What matters in real life is how we apply our knowledge when faced with a problem.

Too many students fail to understand that there's a distinction between learning and getting an education. They think learning only takes place in the context of school and end up missing out on incredible learning opportunities in the real world.

I have been facing real life problems since my childhood. At the age of 13, I had to go alone to Europe in pursuit of science. Since there was no one to advise me, I had to rely on reading scientific magazines and books and asking questions to expand my horizon of knowledge. I had the attitude even at that age that the more I learned from difficult experiences, the stronger I would become. I knew it would help me to be better equipped to deal with future challenges.

If you don't learn anything else from this book, the one thing I want to pass onto you is:

> **TRY TO LEARN FROM EVERYONE AND EVERYTHING IN YOUR LIFE JOURNEY.**

This requires a very open mindset, especially when you're doing things or talking to people who you don't find yourself particularly interested in. But hey, if you find yourself in a situation where you have to be doing something, you might as well take something from it as well.

5.1 WHY YOU SHOULD EXPAND YOUR LEARNING CAPACITY

> THE MIND IS LIKE AN ICEBERG,
> IT FLOATS WITH ONE-SEVENTH OF ITS BULK ABOVE WATER.
> —SIGMUND FREUD (1856 – 1939), THE "FATHER OF PSYCHOANALYSIS".

So why should you expand your learning capacity? This is important to answer, and here is my response: When we gain or earn new knowledge, it lays the foundation to solve the next problem or learn the next new skill, and so on. This enables us to become better problem solvers in life. Thomas Edison had to make 10,000 attempts before he reached his defined goal of inventing a light bulb. As part of this process, he carefully documented each attempt in order to expand his knowledge. This expanded his capacity to learn. He applied his newly gained knowledge to solve the next problem. When I was at university, every lecture provided new information. My brain was loaded with facts or bits of knowledge that accumulated over time.

I had to memorize a lot of facts. What I found useful was that my capacity to learn improved with every problem I solved or assignment I completed. Each semester, my performance improved as I completed new projects and assignments. I increased my fluid intelligence or my capacity to learn new information.

5.2 Practical Steps to Expand Your Learning Capacity

I applied three primary methods to increase my fluid intelligence or reasoning ability.

Fluid intelligence is the general ability to think abstractly, reason, identify patterns, solve problems, and recognize relationships.

In my experience, it is simple to implement practical steps in everyday life to enhance our cognitive ability. My ten years of experience in studying at university supports these steps. Follow them and I promise you will see big improvement in your learning ability.

I apply these three practical proven steps in my life:

1. Seek new activities
2. Think creatively
3. Socialize

5.2.1 Seek New Activities

Great minds are constantly seeking out new activities or learning a new field. When you start a new activity a neuron connection (nerve cell link) is created. These connections build on each other, increasing your neural activity, and creating more connections to build on other connections. In other words, learning is taking place. Geniuses like Einstein and Leonardo da Vinci were skilled in multiple fields. Constantly exposing yourself to new things helps put your brain in a primed state for learning. Always look to new activities to engage your mind and expand your reasoning horizons. Learn an instrument. Take an art class. Go to a museum. Try a new sport. Read about a new area of science. Learn a new language.

When it comes to work, think like Edison:

> "I HAVE NOT FAILED. I'VE JUST FOUND 10,000 WAYS THAT WON'T WORK."

5.2.2. THINK CREATIVELY

I have faced many challenges in my life since childhood. Having a creative mindset was one of the most useful tools I had to face these challenges.

In this section, I will show you how to develop a creative mindset and how to approach challenges. This skill will help you in your personal and professional life.

Creativity can be nurtured. Although you may suddenly get inspired and have a burst of creativity, creativity doesn't have to hit you like a bolt of lightning. It can also be sustained and even enhanced if you have the right attitude.

Creativity is a numbers game. Creative people tend to be prolific, and usually, the misfires far outnumber the hits.

A good example is the artist Picasso. He created about 50,000 works, and not all of them were masterpieces.

It's a powerful lesson: Accept failure. Enjoy it even. Embrace the failure, for the failure is part of the creativity process.

I have put together four tips for expanding your creativity:

1. Keep a notebook and pencil on hand at all times or use the note pad on your phone.

You never know when ideas may hit you. By keeping a notebook around, you will always be able to capture your ideas at any time of the day.

Leonardo da Vinci was well known for keeping a journal of his ideas. His notebooks hold many creative and genius thoughts of this master engineer, painter, and inventor.

His notebooks were filled with plans for flying machines, a parachute, a helicopter, the bicycle, folding furniture, and a number of automated tools for increasing productivity.

A white sheet of paper is the start of a creative and curious mind. The simple act of writing gets you into a creative flow that can last for hours.

2. The second key to creativity is to ask questions or be curious.

Questions are the root of all knowledge and creativity. By continually asking questions about the world around us, we fuel our creative fire. Great minds are those that have asked the greatest questions.

A very good example is Leonardo da Vinci. He asked questions such as: "Why does the thunder last a longer time than that which causes it?" and "Why is the sky blue?"

Socrates asked such questions as: "What is wisdom?" and "What is beauty?"

As a boy, Albert Einstein asked himself, "What would it be like to run beside a light beam at the speed of light?"

By asking questions, we increase our level of consciousness and our view of the world.

3. To become creative, you must also be a hungry reader.

Reading enhances your mental ability and lets you experience the world from a brand new perspective.

When we read a book, we let go of our own perspective and experience the world through the characters that have been crafted by the author.

In my personal experience, I found that the more I read, the better I became at school in later years. Toward the end of my first year of university, I wanted to know more and read more. Reading becomes an unquenchable thirst.

4. Become a big-picture thinker.

In most cases, people are either analytical thinkers who enjoy math, science, and logic, or they are highly imaginative and creative individuals who focus on the big picture.

Our school systems generally accommodate those who are analytical thinkers. This has created employees who are very good at following instructions, but who are not so good at developing new ideas.

Try brainstorming. When seeking a solution to a problem, simply sit down in a quiet, comfortable place and have a pen and paper handy to write down ideas that come to your mind. Don't evaluate, just create. Sit down with others and combine your ideas. You will get more ideas that way.

5.2.3 Socialize

Socializing enhances your mental ability and lets you experience the world from a brand new perspective. It is like reading a book.

When I was a child living by myself in a huge Red Cross camp, I had little knowledge about how to take care of my own daily needs. By socializing with people who were mainly older than me, I managed to retain knowledge and ask questions. I managed to improve my condition by gaining information. By exposing myself to new people, ideas, and environments, I was opening my mind up to new opportunities for cognitive growth. I was also able to get another perspective on the things I had planned to do. This second opinion approach enabled me to be aware of potential dangers. Learning is all about exposing yourself to new things and taking in that information in ways that are meaningful.

5.3 Presentation Skills

Presentation is part of your job as a student in school, college or university, and life after school. I myself had a huge problem with this because I was shy and got nervous when I was standing in front of an audience. The idea of a presentation is to clearly present your message in an enjoyable way so that your audience gets the idea.

Here are the two magic words:

- Preparation
- Confidence

Delivering a presentation to audiences can be a daunting task. You're on stage; all eyes are on you; the audience has high expectations or they wouldn't be there. Every word, your appearance, the tone of your voice and the content of your presentation will be examined in every way.

In my days at university, I learned that:

Fail to prepare = prepare to fail

Preparation is key to giving a good presentation because preparation builds confidence. I have learned to make effective presentations through the following steps, and you will benefit immensely if you follow these steps as well.

Steps in delivering an effective presentation:

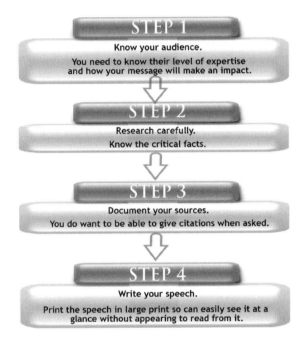

STEP 1
Know your audience.
You need to know their level of expertise and how your message will make an impact.

STEP 2
Research carefully.
Know the critical facts.

STEP 3
Document your sources.
You do want to be able to give citations when asked.

STEP 4
Write your speech.
Print the speech in large print so can easily see it at a glance without appearing to read from it.

STEP 5

Prepare the slide show.

The visuals you will show to the audience need to be designed to support what you are saying. Avoid showing a slide that has lots of details. Remember the visulas are for impact

On bullet slides, set up the slide to start blank and to add bullets one by one only after a button click.

STEP 6

Practice alone.

Practice repeatedly. Read your speech and watch your presentation dozens of times.

Know what comes next

STEP 7

Do a try-out.

Ask people you trust to give honest opinions. These should be people that are reasonably representative of your expected audience.

STEP 8

Prepare yourself.

Find a quiet spot, close your eyes, and go over the presentation.

5.4 Team work Skills

TEAM stands for: Together Everyone Achieves More.

Life is a series of team projects. Knowing how to be a good team player will save you a lot of energy. Group assignments are set to prepare you for your professional future, to give you a chance to tackle significant projects, and to enable you to demonstrate teamwork skills in your resume.

In most disciplines in university or college, you will encounter group assignments. Generally this is a compulsory part of your course. Students who are new to this approach sometimes feel anxious about managing the group work process.

Some of the problems that students encounter are:

- Misunderstandings about responsibilities.
- Lack of commitment in some group members.
- Personality clashes.
- One person doing all the work.

In an effective team, members compensate for each other's weaknesses.

From my many years of teamwork and group assignment experiences, I have compiled strategies that you can use to make sure your team runs smoothly and achieves a successful outcome.

1. Be reliable and consistent.

You can count on a reliable team member who gets work done and does his or her fair share to meet commitments and follow through on assignments. Consistency is key. You can count on him or her to deliver good performance all the time and not just some of the time.

2. Communicate constructively.

In other words, express your suggestions without implying a negative message. Teams need people who speak up and express their thoughts and ideas clearly, directly, honestly, and with respect for others and for the work of the team. That's what it means to communicate constructively. Such a team member does not shy away from making a point, but makes it in the best way. Approach team members in a positive, confident, and respectful manner.

3. Listen actively.

Teams need team players who can absorb, understand, and consider ideas and points of view from other people without debating and arguing every point. Such a team member also can receive criticism without reacting defensively. Most importantly, for effective communication and problem solving, team members need the discipline to listen first and speak second so that meaningful dialogue results.

4. Share openly and willingly.

Good team players share. They're willing to share information, knowledge, and experience. They take the initiative to keep other team members informed.

5. Be flexible.

Teams often deal with changing conditions—and often create changes themselves. Good team players roll with the punches; they adapt to ever-changing situations. They don't complain or get stressed out because something new is being tried or some new direction is being set. Strong team players are firm in their thoughts yet open to what others have to offer—flexibility at its best.

6. WORK AS A PROBLEM-SOLVER.

Teams, of course, deal with problems. Often that's the whole reason why a team is created—to address problems. Good team players are willing to deal with all kinds of problems in a solutions-oriented manner. They're problem-solvers, not problem-dwellers, problem-blamers, or problem-avoiders. They don't look for others to fault, as the blamers do, and they don't put off dealing with issues, the way avoiders do. Team players get problems out in the open for discussion and then collaborate with others to find solutions and form action plans.

7. TREAT OTHERS IN A RESPECTFUL AND SUPPORTIVE MANNER.

Team players treat fellow team members with courtesy and consideration—not just some of the time but consistently. In addition, they show understanding and the appropriate support of other team members to help get the job done.

Good team players also have a sense of humor and know how to have fun. Simply, effective team players deal with other people in a professional manner.

5.5 HOW TO UNDERSTAND A CONCEPT

Most students push themselves to memorize facts and information that enable them to get the mark they need to go to the next stage. I have encountered many students who memorize a lot, get the mark, and then forget the information after a short period of time. They mainly use their short-term memory to get through the test, and afterwards, nothing is there to help them with future problems. Why not learn something that later on in life helps you with your problem solving skills.

Long-term memory is associated with intelligence. It is important that by understanding the concepts or main ideas you expand your long-term memory. This will assist you to be a better problem solver in the future.

I want you to take note of an important study technique. Try focusing on getting the main idea behind a science concept. I have devised a simple method called "WEA".

> **W:** Write the concept.
>
> **E:** Explain it to yourself in writing.
>
> **A:** Analogize. That is, make a comparison with something else to assist you in understanding.

Let's look at an example of applying this method: Understanding torque.

In physics, this concept helps make life easier. If you want to remove a bolt, you use a wrench. You can move a boulder better if you have a long pole.

W: Write down the concept. Torque.

E: Explain it to yourself.

Torque is an influence that tends to change the rotational motion of an object. One way to quantify torque is:

Torque = Force applied x lever arm

A: Analogize.

Make a comparison with a tool in life. You can remove a bolt by using a wrench.

Let's try another example: Acceleration.

Just imagine yourself standing in a bus and holding onto the pole when a sudden force makes you lean forward or backwards.

When you seek analogy for this concept, try using Google and type in: "Analogy acceleration"

You will get loads of images. Study them and give yourself time to understand it.

5.6 Practice Self-education

> *Self-education is, I firmly believe, the only kind of education there is.*
> —Isaac Asimov (1920 – 1992) was one of the most prolific science fiction writers of all time. He has more than 500 books to his credit.

Today the classroom is no longer the only option for receiving an education. Anybody with an interest and an Internet connection can receive an education. Learning has become more interesting, since people now have the freedom to choose what to learn, and this is helping to spread knowledge around the world.

You have the potential to develop knowledge and skills that will far outweigh the things you would learn just by attending school. The great thing about self-education is that there are no grades, no tests, or requirements. It's purely about the joy of learning, and you can learn at your own pace.

5.6.1 Eight Techniques that Stimulate Self-education

1. Learn how to make an observation: Use a notebook to take note of what is important. By counting the number of repetitive events and making a sketch, you can filter the important factors from the less important parts. Let's take the example of the

cucumber in the garden. You notice that some cucumbers are bigger than others and wonder why. Because of this experience and an interest in the problem, you decide to learn more about what makes some cucumbers grow larger.

2. Question something: Open-minded and informed questions can help you to comprehend information placed before you, as well as take out information useful to you. Ask questions such as: How can this observation be explained? Why does this work the way it does? Can it be done in any other way?

3. Review a question based on observation and data: Once you have stated and noted your questions and answers, go back and review your notes and data. This relates to collecting project data in a consistent, systematic manner (i.e., reliability) and establishing an ongoing system for evaluating and recording changes in your recorded information.

4. Draw a conclusion: When you form a conclusion, you make a decision after considering all facts. It is better not to draw a conclusion if you don't have all the information. The following tips may help you to draw conclusions:

    - Make connections between pieces of information.

    - Look into your past knowledge or consult a trusted, well-informed source.

    - Understand if your past knowledge applies to the current situation.

5. Explain the significance: The significance of something refers to its meaning and importance with regards to consequences. For instance, ask yourself: What happens if this factor is removed from the equation? Something that carries weight in an argument, story, or an observation.

6. Transfer a lesson or philosophical stance from one situation to another: Transfer is the ability to extend what one has learned in one context to new contexts. In some sense, the whole point of school learning is to be able to transfer what is learned there to a wide variety of contexts outside of school. Yet the ability to transfer information or ideas is not a given.

   Improving intelligence requires the ability to transfer lessons from one situation to another. This enables one to perform better. Thus, it is important to understand the concepts, rather than memorizing facts and getting the required marks only to forget everything soon afterwards. So remember, try to get the main idea behind any information that is presented to you.

7. Identify a cause and effect: A cause is *why* an event took place, and an effect is *what happened* as a result. The following steps will enable you to identify a cause:

   - Look for signs that point to the existence of a cause-and-effect relationship.

   - Identify the relationship. Find out how events are connected.

   - Be aware of complex connections, and look beyond the immediate or superficial cause and effect for deeper, less apparent connections.

8. Learn to identify a pattern: Finding a pattern in data is a strategy that can sometimes be used to solve a problem. In this process, one must look for items, numbers, or a series of events that are repeated. Here is a simple way to find a pattern:

   - Collect data. Gather as much information as you can.

   - Observe the data. At this stage, you can break down the information into small, manageable groups.

- Ask questions and look for solutions. Ask yourself why some information appears as it does. Look for repeated data. Brainstorm for possible solutions.

Extract lessons from nature. Observing nature can teach us a thing or two. After all, nature has been around longer on this earth than we have. For example, we can learn a lesson about flexibility from nature. If you have ever experienced an ice storm or heavy snow, observing trees will show you that only the trees with highly flexible branches managed to avoid destruction. Here is an example that I observed during a recent ice storm.

Tree hit by ice storm, Day 1

Tree hit by ice storm, Day 5

Tree hit by ice storm, Day 10

5.6.2 Resources for Self-education

Practice self-education by seeking the following resources:

- Local library: When you are in a library, your curiosity kicks in and you want to look at books. Find an easy skill to learn, and look for related books and materials. This will get you into the habit of doing research.

- YouTube: Video is an easy way to learn things. Type your key words and lay back and watch. I managed to learn how to do many of my plumbing repair jobs from YouTube—so can you.

- Online courses: There are a number of universities, colleges, and educational institutions offering online courses. Depending on your needs, contact them and ask for courses related to your interest.

- Seminars: Attend seminars in your field of interest, and you will get the knowledge without taking long courses that make you feel tired and overloaded.

5.7 How Great Minds Viewed Learning

I am not afraid of storms for
I am learning how to sail my ship.
—Louisa May Alcott (1832 – 1888) was an American novelist and author of *Little Women* in 1868. She is a good example of how self-education can activate the creative part of the human mind. She received the majority of her education from her father and the poet Ralph Waldo Emerson.

> LEARNING NEVER EXHAUSTS THE MIND.
> —LEONARDO DA VINCI (1452 – 1519) was an Italian enigmatic genius from the 16th century. When we hear his name, we associate it mainly with art. But in my understanding of him, he was also a master engineer. He regarded himself more as an inventor who invented methods to harness the power of nature. He produced more than 6,000 pages of documents, which today confirm his reputation as "genius".

> I HAVE NEVER MET A MAN SO IGNORANT
> THAT I COULDN'T LEARN SOMETHING FROM HIM.
> —GALILEO GALILEI (1564 – 1642) was an Italian physicist, mathematician, and astronomer. He was the father of modern science. His observations of the natural world paved the way for great achievement in science.

....

The above quote is a reminder that with an open mind we can overcome the unpleasantness of dealing with a difficult person and focus on the things we can learn.

> EDUCATION IS WHAT REMAINS AFTER ONE
> HAS FORGOTTEN WHAT ONE HAS LEARNED IN SCHOOL.
> —ALBERT EINSTEIN (1879 – 1955) was a Nobel Prize-winning, German-born theoretical physicist who established the general theory of relativity. He published more than 300 scientific papers.

....

The above quote indicates that real life learning starts after school. We educate ourselves by interacting with our surroundings. We retain information more naturally when we do this kind of learning versus schools spoon-feeding the information to us. Self-learning allows learners to interact with the subject matter as deeply as they would like to go.

> I AM ALWAYS DOING THAT WHICH I CANNOT DO,
> IN ORDER THAT I MAY LEARN HOW TO DO IT.
> —PABLO PICASSO (1881 – 1973) WAS A SPANISH PAINTER WHO IS CONSIDERED TO BE ONE OF THE GREATEST ARTISTS OF THE 20TH CENTURY. HE PRODUCED MORE THAN 2,000 PAINTINGS AND MORE THAN 45,000 OTHER PIECES OF ART SUCH AS SCULPTURES, CERAMICS, AND DRAWINGS.

Picasso was always changing his painting style. He expanded his learning capacity by challenging himself with projects that were new to him. He kept up his momentum by constantly switching between projects. This technique is also known to have been used by Edison. This parallel processing approach helped him to beat the boredom and stress of dealing with just one project.

> I AM STILL LEARNING.
> —MICHELANGELO (1475 – 1564) WAS AN ITALIAN SCULPTOR, PAINTER, ARCHITECT, POET, AND ENGINEER. HE IS CONSIDERED TO BE ONE OF THE GREATEST ARTISTS OF ALL TIME.

Michelangelo viewed learning as a path to other successes. His ability to work intensely and learn from many projects earned him vast knowledge and that enabled him to apply his learning to new projects. This approach played a key role in his wonderful accomplishments. This is a confirmation that the capacity to learn has no limit, and we decide how deeply we want to explore our capacity.

> I AM ALWAYS READY TO LEARN ALTHOUGH
> I DO NOT ALWAYS LIKE BEING TAUGHT.
> —WINSTON CHURCHILL (1874 – 1965) WAS AN ENGLISH STATESMAN WHO WAS AWARDED THE NOBEL PRIZE IN LITERATURE. WINSTON CHURCHILL WAS A SKILLED ARTIST AND TOOK GREAT PLEASURE IN PAINTING. HE ALSO WAS AN EXCELLENT WRITER.

> People usually think according to their inclinations,
> speak according to their learning and ingrained opinions,
> but generally act according to custom.
> —Francis Bacon (1561 – 1626) was an English philosopher, statesman, and scientist.

Bacon invented a scientific method (the Bacon method), which consists of techniques for investigating phenomena, acquiring new knowledge, and/or correcting and integrating previous knowledge. It is interesting to see that what we learn will affect the way we communicate with our environment.

5.8 My Experience

In my experience, learning subjects that are interesting to you energizes your mind. Learning does not need to be school material. It can be anything that you need at the present time.

In the process of learning, the mind stays sharp and the old garbage that bothers us due to the day-to-day challenges of life gets flushed out. Even feeling good for few hours in the course of leaning is a reward. Consider learning as mental floss for yourself.

Exercises

Exercise 1: *Make a list of the top ten new activities that interest you and that you plan to do in the next 6 months.*

1
2

3 ....

4 ....

5 ....

6 ....

7 ....

8 ....

9 ....

10 ....

Exercise 2: *List the top ten places where you can socialize and find friends with common interests.*

1 ....

2 ....

3 ....

4 ....

5 ....

6 ....

7 ....

8 ....

9 ....

10 ....

Exercise 3: *Write down ten examples of when you came up with a creative solution to a problem.*

1 ....
2 ....
3 ....
4 ....
5 ....
6 ....
7 ....
8 ....
9 ....
10 ....

Exercise 4: *What creative solutions did you come up with when faced with a challenge?*

1 ....
2 ....
3 ....
4 ....
5 ....
6 ....
7 ....
8 ....

9 ....

10 ....

Exercise 5: *Practice my "WEA" method for understanding by selecting five concepts in physics and finding analogies for them.*

1 ....

2 ....

3 ....

4 ....

5 ....

Sixth Key:
How to Approach a Problem

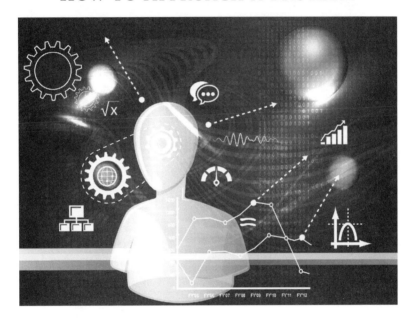

IT IS A COMMON EXPERIENCE THAT
A PROBLEM DIFFICULT AT NIGHT IS RESOLVED IN THE
MORNING AFTER THE COMMITTEE OF SLEEP
HAS WORKED ON IT.
—John Steinbeck (1902 – 1968), writer.

Topics in this section:

- The Power of Your Subconscious Mind

- How to Approach Math and Physics Problems
- Ask the Three Questions
- How to Approach a Project
- Critical Thinking Skills
- How Great Minds Viewed Problems

Introduction

You will encounter problems in your career as a student and in daily life. When I was studying for my engineering degree, I once complained to one of my professors about the workload of assignments and technical problems. He simply said, "Dealing with these problems will make you an engineer."

Developing the attitude and tools to deal with problems will shape your career and life after school because no matter where you go, there will be a need for problem solvers. In this section, I will point out the approaches that proved to be successful in my days at university. I still employ these techniques for day-to-day problems in my life.

6.1 The Power of Your Subconscious Mind

> When I am traveling in a carriage, or walking after a good meal, or during the night when I cannot sleep; it is on such occasions that ideas flow best and most abundantly.
> —Wolfgang Amadeus Mozart (1756 – 1791), composer.

I will share a secret with you that will give you the edge to becoming a superstar student: Harness the power of the subconscious mind.

When I was studying for my Mechanical Engineering degree in Denmark, solving math and physics problems proved to be a major challenge. That is, until one day a fantastic professor at the university told me to harness the power of my subconscious mind. Initially I didn't pay any attention, but after a while, I decided to apply this technique. One night, after working unsuccessfully on a problem for 2 hours, I decided to continue it in the morning. To my surprise, after opening the book and looking at the problem the next day, the solution streamed into my mind. Yes, it is true.

I know many colleagues who got solutions to their challenging engineering problems when taking a shower or watering the garden.

Many scientists, engineers, composers, and historical figures attribute their success to the power of the subconscious. They all maintain that solutions appeared, not when they were working on the problem consciously, but when they were engaged in some undemanding activity. The people who frequently tap into the subconscious for answers know there is no such thing as "impossible". The term "impossible" comes from our lack of awareness of our vast potential.

Our subconscious mind is like a muscle. The more you train it, the stronger it becomes. Ancient Egyptians had access to subconscious power, and it helped them to build the pyramids. Most people do not know that they hold this vast storehouse of knowledge within, and therefore, do not look to it for answers—at least not consciously.

Again I want to emphasize that the term "impossible" comes from our unawareness.

6.2 How to Practice Subconscious Problem Solving

There are some simple ways to activate the problem-solving gear of the subconscious. Once you know how to use them efficiently, you have an additional tool to help you become an excellent problem solver.

Mindless activities that I do to boost my subconscious power are:

- Walking
- Taking a shower
- Watering the lawn
- Listening to music
- Washing and folding the laundry
- Cleaning and putting away dishes
- Sweeping the floors

6.3 How to Approach Math and Physics Problems

This is how I approached the seemingly unsolvable math and physics problems I encountered in university:

1. Find a quiet place to focus.
2. Read the problem.
3. Review the textbook and examples. Most physics and math textbooks have a lesson to read. Read it word by word.
4. Go to YouTube and the Internet to find examples.

5. Write down all the steps in solving the problem.

6. In your own words, write down the description of the problem.

7. Write down all the known facts in a corner of the paper and draw a box around it.

8. Write down all the unknown facts in another corner and draw a box around it.

9. Determine what the problem is asking you to solve.

10. Solve the problem.

11. Check your answer.

12. If you are unable to solve the problem, spend 10 minutes visualizing the problem before you go to bed that night.

13. In the morning, go directly to the problem and you should have the answer.

What if you come back and say, "Hey, I still don't have a solution"?

Here comes the fundamental work. Don't give up until you get it. That's part of working on your persistence skills as covered in the previous sections.

6.4 Ask the Three Questions

When I was a student in the third year of my engineering studies, I was introduced to a problem solving tool that has served me well.

When faced with an assignment I ask three questions:

1. What is the problem?

2. Why is that a problem?

3. How can the problem be solved?

1. What is the problem?

The problem may not be obvious. Identifying *what* the problem is usually solves 50% of the problem. This step may take a while since it is always hard to correctly identify the issues. I did the following to correctly identify the problem:

- Write down the problem in your own words.
- Write down the unknown.

2. Why is that a problem?

Once you identify the problem, you can focus on the elements that caused the problem and start identifying possible solutions. In order for me to get an overview of the problem, I would:

- Make a list of causes that led to the problem.
- Stay calm and logical when approaching the problem.

3. How can the problem be solved?

At this stage, I would begin to give structure to the process of finding a path to the solution. This might be doing research on the subject or finding a similar case, learning from it, and applying it to my area of focus. I did the following steps to help with my search for the solution:

- Brainstorm
- Research
- Ask a question from an expert in the field.

6.5 How to Approach a Project

In the course of your academic and everyday life you will encounter projects. Whether it is writing a research paper or building a shed, you can save yourself a lot of time and energy by learning a simple project management skill called TBS (Task Breakdown Structure).

One trick to get the momentum going to start a project is breaking the job down into smaller tasks.

This technique is used in engineering projects and learning it will help you to be more efficient in school. This is one of the many useful skills in this chapter that I think will give you an edge in becoming a successful student.

A way to break down projects is to set milestones and do a rough estimation of how long it will take to reach them. Don't over-complicate things. Usually project planning and estimates are unreliable in the beginning of a project. But as you go along, estimates and plans improve as you get to know what you are completing.

There many advanced and detailed project management techniques such as the Gantt Chart. You will learn these in college or university if it is included in your curriculum.

I decided to include a simple technique that really worked for me in university and with occasional projects in my house. Let's look at an example: You want to read a 100-page book. Then you get the overwhelming feeling that it is too much. Now let's use this approach that I learned when I was studying for Engineering.

1. Set a 5-hour goal to complete the reading within 5 days, starting Monday.

2. Break down the book into 25-page sections for each day's reading time of one hour per day.

3. Read the easiest part.

4. Now you have the momentum.

5. By Thursday, you will have completed the last portion of 25 pages.

6. Allow an extra day for reserve on Friday.

7. Your book-reading project is complete.

You can use this TBS (Task Breakdown Structure) for any academic or other project you encounter. Here is a schematic diagram for the book reading project:

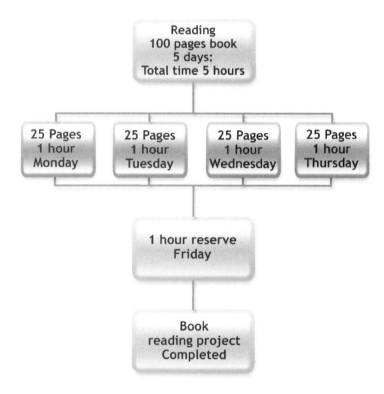

6.6 Critical Thinking Skills

> Critical thinking is a method
> to identify information that makes sense.
> —Mehdi Toozhy

In everyday life we interact with people, read news, go shopping. We constantly face the task of making a selection. Critical thinking skills help me to make an informed decision when I am faced with a selection.

In this section, I will explain some simple techniques that will help you make smarter decisions in everyday life.

Ask the three critical questions:

1. Why is this information presented to me?
2. How can I validate the accuracy of the information?
3. Does it make sense?

When we think, we bring a variety of thoughts together into some order. When the combination of thoughts is mutually supporting and makes sense, the thinking is "logical". When the combination is not mutually supporting, is contradictory in some sense, or does not "make sense", the combination is not logical.

6.7 How Great Minds Viewed Problems

Around us are many tools and devices that can make our daily lives more comfortable. Behind all of these inventions lay many obstacles that inventors had to overcome to reach a solution to their problem. Let's have a look at one of my personal heroes and his approach to problem solving.

6.7.1 Thomas Alva Edison

> *I have not failed.*
> *I've just found 10,000 ways that won't work.*
> —Thomas A. Edison (1847 – 1931), inventor.

This famous quote came from the invention of the light bulb.

Edison approached the problem of inventing a light bulb with immense stamina and systematically took notes for every path towards the solution. He viewed every failure as an opportunity of getting closer to the solution. His knowledge expanded the more he attempted.

I can certify that approach. In the first two years of university, I struggled with problems. By my third year, my ability to solve problems had improved rapidly.

The good news for those of you planning to start university is that after the first two years you will be better at dealing with problems.

Edison's Parallel Processing Approach: Thomas Edison used to work on several problems at the same time. The idea behind it is that if you get stuck with one, you can start working on another problem. Your subconscious mind will accept the new work, but still work on the other problem in the background.

The advantage of this technique is that you won't get tired by constantly looking at the same problem if you get stuck on it.

6.7.2 Albert Einstein

> *It's not that I'm so smart,*
> *it's just that I stay with problems longer.*
> —Albert Einstein (1879 – 1955), theoretical physicist.

This is another example that goes back to a fundamental of problem solving, which is persistence. In a previous chapter, we discussed that persistence is a quality that can be developed.

> WE CANNOT SOLVE OUR PROBLEMS WITH THE SAME THINKING WE USED WHEN WE CREATED THEM.
> —ALBERT EINSTEIN (1879 – 1955), THEORETICAL PHYSICIST.

The above quote implies the need to be open-minded and humble when looking for a solution. Considering other people's views and perspectives will enhance the chance of finding a solution.

6.7.3 HENRY FORD

> MOST PEOPLE SPEND MORE TIME AND ENERGY GOING AROUND PROBLEMS THAN IN TRYING TO SOLVE THEM.
> —HENRY FORD (1863 – 1947) WAS AN AMERICAN INDUSTRIALIST WHO INVENTED THE ASSEMBLY LINE FOR AUTOMOBILE MANUFACTURING.

In my experience, running away from problems deprives you of the opportunity to gain the valuable knowledge that comes with dealing with them.

Recommended reading:

- David J. Schwartz, *The Magic of Thinking Big*
- Elaine St. James, *Simplify Your Life*

Exercises

Exercise 1: *Five minutes before bedtime, write down a problem you need to solve. First thing in the morning, look it up and work on the solution.*

Before bedtime:
....

When you wake up in the morning:
....

Repeat the exercise and make a journal of your results.

Exercise 2: *Make a list of interests and activities (such as chess, computer games, crosswords, etc.) that may be useful in practicing your problem-solving skills.*

1 ....
2 ....
3 ....
4 ....
5 ....
6 ....
7 ....
8 ....
9 ....
10 ....

Exercise 3: *Make a list of your approaches to a problem.*

1 ....

2 ....

3 ....

4 ....

5 ....

6 ....

7 ....

8 ....

9 ....

10 ....

Exercise 4: *Describe a situation in which you analyzed data and solved a complex problem.*

Seventh Key:
How to Discover Your Own Path

> The more intensely we feel about an idea or a goal, the more assuredly the idea, buried deep in our subconscious, will direct us along the path to its fulfillment.
> —Earl Nightingale (1921 – 1989), writer.

....

Topics in this section:

- How to Discover Your Passion

- How Great Minds Discovered Their Paths

Introduction

As a student, there are many things happening in your life. Figuring out what subject to study in college or university can be a daunting task. I have gone through a similar situation, and I will share my knowledge with you so it will be easier for you to find out what you want to do.

7.1 How to Discover Your Passion

Many students find it difficult to decide what subject to study. After all, you will be making a big time and money investment in the program you choose. When I was in grade nine, my school had a work experience internship program for students. Each month, we selected a week of voluntary work in a selected profession. I volunteered for five different professional field placements during the course of that year. They were:

1. Audio/video
2. Engineering consulting
3. Machine tooling
4. Landscaping architect
5. Swimming instructor

Attending the above work places gave me an idea about what I wanted to study in university. Eventually I studied engineering.

So what do we learn from this? Volunteer!

When you volunteer, you can explore your ideas and get a practical sense of what you want to do in the future.

Today, tools to do research are more extensive than before, so you can do an even better job of finding out what career you want to choose.

If you really don't know what to study at university, don't worry. You may choose a subject and later find out that it is not for you. This is all about discovery. Expect disappointment and failure, but look at the failure as learning (as we discussed in previous sections). Remember, you learn from your errors.

I want you to keep my two golden rules in mind:

> WHEN IT COMES TO WORK, THINK LIKE EDISON:
> "I HAVE NOT FAILED. I'VE JUST FOUND 10,000 WAYS THAT WON'T WORK."

> WHEN IT COMES TO PEOPLE, THINK LIKE MOZART:
> "I PAY NO ATTENTION WHATEVER TO ANYBODY'S PRAISE OR BLAME. I SIMPLY FOLLOW MY OWN FEELINGS."

....

When discovering your passion, you need to find a quiet space and ask yourself the following questions:

- What makes me burn less energy to achieve my goal?
- What activity energizes me?
- What helps me to stand up in the morning and move towards my daily goals?

I recommend these three simple steps to discover your passion:

1. Brainstorm: As discussed before, you can put your mind into neutral and let it generate ideas. Write them down on a piece of paper.

2. Evaluate your ideas with a trusted professional source. This can be anybody who your school recommends and/or do your own research by:

- Finding a professional interview on YouTube or elsewhere on the Internet.

- Going to the library and reading books about the subject you are considering studying.

- Asking successful people for their opinion on your ideas.

3. Make a plan: This plan can be from the moment you find out what you want to do. Every step that you take should bring you closer to your goal (for example, selecting a field of study for college or university). Even your day-to-day life can be geared toward achieving your goal. For example, be aware of expenses related to your weekend entertainment. The more money you save, the more you can focus on your studies at school. So give your plan the following dimensions: Time, money, and commitment.

> DOES ANYBODY REALLY THINK THAT THEY DIDN'T GET WHAT THEY HAD BECAUSE THEY DIDN'T HAVE THE TALENT OR THE STRENGTH OR THE ENDURANCE OR THE COMMITMENT?
> —NELSON MANDELA (1918 – 2013), ANTI-APARTHEID ACTIVIST, HUMANIST, AND PHILANTHROPIST.

For example, if you want to become an engineer, your plan should be for 4 years and budget the money you need to let you focus on your studies. Then comes the commitment. You have to ask yourself:

1. Do you have the patience to stay on course?

2. Can I learn the skills to deal with many ups and down?

Once you follow the steps in this section to find your interest, meeting challenges is what will make your character. In times of difficulty, read

Fourth Key: Don't Give Up. That should enable you to get on the wagon again in your path to become what you chose to be.

7.2 How Great Minds Discovered Their Paths

I have observed many great minds' accomplishments, and I have selected a few to show you that once you start your passion, work will become more enjoyable and you will be surprised as you discover your capabilities.

> I've come to believe that each of us has a personal calling that's as unique as a fingerprint—and that the best way to succeed is to discover what you love and then find a way to offer it to others in the form of service, working hard, and also allowing the energy of the universe to lead you.
> —Oprah Winfrey, talk show host, actress, producer, and philanthropist. She is a good example of what one can achieve by pursuing work through passion.

> Choose a job you love, and you will never have to work a day in your life.
> —Confucius (551 BC – 479 BC) was a Chinese philosopher who supported strong family values and respect of elders by their children. He contributed to Chinese classic textbooks. His teachings had a basis in common Chinese tradition and belief.

> Opportunity is missed by most people because it is dressed in overalls and looks like work.
> —Thomas A. Edison (1847 – 1931) was an American inventor with more than one thousand patents. His inventions revolutionized many industries worldwide. Just the invention of the electric light bulb and an electricity distribution system improved the life of humanity.

> Everyone has been made for some particular work, and the desire for that work has been put in every heart.
> —Mawlana (1207 – 1273) was a 13th-century Persian poet and philosopher. His many works, such as six masterpiece books of the Masnavis, contributed immensely to the spiritual evolution of human beings.

> Pleasure in the job puts perfection in the work.
> —Aristotle (384 BC – 322 BC) was a Greek philosopher and scientist. This true genius had a sea of accomplishments. One of his major contributions was the establishment of scientific methods, such as logic. He contributed immensely in many fields of human knowledge.

> Love and work are the cornerstones of our humanness.
> —Sigmund Freud (1856 – 1939) was an Austrian psychiatrist who became known as the "Founding Father of Psychoanalysis". His deep scientific research into the human mind continues to influence many areas of modern culture.

> Work is love made visible. And if you cannot work with love but only with distaste, it is better that you should leave your work and sit at the gate of the temple and take alms of those who work with joy.
> —Khalil Gibran (1883 – 1931) was a Lebanese artist and poet. He is credited with more than 700 drawings and watercolor. He considered himself a citizen of earth. He contributed immensely to modern Arabic literature.

> It is your work in life that is the ultimate seduction.
> —Pablo Picasso (1881 – 1973) was a Spanish artist who is credited with more than 50,000 paintings and is considered to be one of the most influential artists of the 20th century. It is said that his best paintings are those that deeply touched his heart.

> A SUCCESSFUL LIFE IS ONE THAT IS LIVED THROUGH UNDERSTANDING AND PURSUING ONE'S OWN PATH, NOT CHASING AFTER THE DREAMS OF OTHERS.
> —CHIN-NING CHU (1947 – 2009) WAS A CHINESE-AMERICAN BUSINESSWOMAN AND A SUCCESSFUL BUSINESS MANAGEMENT AUTHOR IN ASIA AND THE PACIFIC RIM.

> YOU:
> "I, THE READER (BIRTH DATE TO ...), PRESENT IN THIS UNIVERSE, HAVE RECEIVED THE MESSAGE TO MOVE THIS CIVILIZATION FORWARD STARTING WITH ME."

7.3 EINSTEIN SECRET MESSAGE TO HIS SON

In 1915 Einstein completed his historical masterpiece, the two-page theory of general relativity. He sent his 11-year-old son Hans Albert a letter, found in the book Posterity by Dorie Mccullough Lawson: Letters of Great Americans to Their Children:

"You are doing something with such enjoyment that you don't notice that the time passes"

So here is a very important lesson for you:

Find a profession that you are passionate about.

EXERCISES

Exercise 1: *Write down ten activities that energize you.*

1 ....

2 ....

3 ....

4
....

5
....

6
....

7
....

8
....

9
....

10
....

Exercise 2: *List the ten most appealing professions to you.*

1
....

2
....

3
....

4
....

5
....

6
....

7
....

8
....

9
....

10
....

Exercise 3: *Make a list of the top ten universities or colleges and research their admission requirements.*

1
....

2 ....

3 ....

4 ....

5 ....

6 ....

7 ....

8 ....

9 ....

10 ....

Exercise 4: *Test your critical thinking skills when you are approached by a salesperson.*

Ask yourself the following:

1. Why is this product being presented to me?

2. How can I validate the accuracy of the information?

3. Does it help me?

References

Almond Board of California. (n.d.). Retrieved from http://www.almonds.com

Aristotle — Wikipedia, the free encyclopedia. (n.d.). Retrieved June 8, 2014, from http://en.wikipedia.org/wiki/Aristotle

Canfield, J., Hansen, M. V., and Hewitt, L. (2000). *The Power of Focus.* Deerfield Beach, Florida: Health Communications.

Cheetah — Wikipedia, the free encyclopedia. (n.d.). Retrieved June 8, 2014, from http://en.wikipedia.org/wiki/Cheetah

Clark, R. (1977). *Edison: The Man Who Made the Future.* New York: Putnam.

Commitment Quotes — BrainyQuote. (n.d.). Retrieved from http://www.brainyquote.com/quotes/keywords/commitment.html

Cougar — Wikipedia, the free encyclopedia. (n.d.). Retrieved June 8, 2014, from http://en.wikipedia.org/wiki/Cougar#Hunting_and_diet

Critical thinking — Wikipedia, the free encyclopedia. (n.d.). Retrieved June 8, 2014, from http://en.wikipedia.org/wiki/Critical_thinking

Ed Parker — Wikipedia, the free encyclopedia. (n.d.). Retrieved June 8, 2014, from http://en.wikipedia.org/wiki/Ed_Parker

Elbert Hubbard — Wikipedia, the free encyclopedia. (n.d.). Retrieved June 8, 2014, from http://en.wikipedia.org/wiki/Elbert_Hubbard

"Family, not area, is key to a child's education: Children with parents who spent extra year in education get better grades". *Mail Online*. (n.d.). Retrieved from http://www.dailymail.co.uk/news/article-2303716/Family-area-key-childs-education-Children-parents-spent-extra-year-education-better-grades.html?ito=feeds-newsxml

Gardner, H. (1983). *Frames of mind: The Theory of Multiple Intelligences*. New York: Basic Books.

Golden eagle — Wikipedia, the free encyclopedia. (n.d.). Retrieved June 8, 2014, from http://en.wikipedia.org/wiki/Golden_Eagle

Great white shark — Wikipedia, the free encyclopedia. (n.d.). Retrieved June 8, 2014, from http://en.wikipedia.org/wiki/Great_white_shark

"Health & Nutrition",| Almond Board of California. (n.d.). Retrieved from http://www.almonds.com/consumers/health-and-nutrition#tc-nutrition

Kahlil Gibran — Wikipedia, the free encyclopedia. (n.d.). Retrieved June 8, 2014, from http://en.wikipedia.org/wiki/Kahlil_Gibran

Killer whale — Wikipedia, the free encyclopedia. (n.d.). Retrieved June 8, 2014, from http://en.wikipedia.org/wiki/Killer_whale

Landrus, M. (2006). *Treasures of Leonardo da Vinci*. New York, NY: HarperCollins.

Leopard — Wikipedia, the free encyclopedia. (n.d.). Retrieved June 8, 2014, from http://en.wikipedia.org/wiki/Leopard

Lion — Wikipedia, the free encyclopedia. (n.d.). Retrieved June 8, 2014, from http://en.wikipedia.org/wiki/Lion

Michelangelo — Wikipedia, the free encyclopedia. (n.d.). Retrieved June 8, 2014, from http://en.wikipedia.org/wiki/Michelangelo

Novella, S., Hidenrick, T., Leven, J., and Teaching Company (2012). *Your Deceptive Mind: A Scientific Guide to Critical Thinking Skills.* Chantilly, Virginia: Teaching Company.

"Nutrition — California Walnuts". (n.d.). Retrieved from http://www.walnuts.org/health-and-walnuts/nutrition/

Rumi — Wikipedia, the free encyclopedia. (n.d.). Retrieved June 8, 2014, from http://en.wikipedia.org/wiki/Rumi

Sternberg, R. (n.d.). "Increasing fluid intelligence is possible after all." National Academy of Sciences.

"This column will change your life: Self-perception theory". *The Guardian.* (n.d.). Retrieved from http://www.theguardian.com/lifeandstyle/2012/oct/05/change-your-life-self-perception-theory

Tiger — Wikipedia, the free encyclopedia. (n.d.). Retrieved June 8, 2014, from http://en.wikipedia.org/wiki/Tiger

Weinberg, R. A. (1989). "Intelligence and IQ: Landmark Issues and Great Debates". *American Psychologist.* doi:10.1037/0003-066X.44.2.98

Printed in Canada